EMSWORTH

A History

The cupola and clock of the former St Peter's Chapel is a well known Emsworth landmark.

EMSWORTH
A History

Robert Whitfield

Phillimore

2005

Published by
PHILLIMORE & CO. LTD
Shopwyke Manor Barn, Chichester, West Sussex, England

ISBN 1 86077 346 X

Printed and bound in Great Britain by
CAMBRIDGE PRINTING

For Sarah

Contents

List of Illustrations

Frontispiece: St Peter's chapel cupola and clock

Acknowledgements

My thanks are due to many individuals and organisations for their help with my research. Staff at the Hampshire Record Office, Portsmouth Central Library, Portsmouth City Record Office, West Sussex Record Office and the British Library (Newspaper Collection) have all helped to make my task easier through the professional way in which they have dealt with my requests and queries. I am also grateful to the staff of the Havant Museum, the Emsworth Branch Library and the Imperial War Museum.

I am grateful to Roy and Sheila Morgan, archivists of the Emsworth Maritime and Historical Trust, for taking the time to answer my queries. My thanks are also due to Mr Gerry Daly for giving me permission to use his unpublished University of Portsmouth dissertation. My friend Barry Fogden has given support and helpful advice throughout this project and made many helpful observations on the first draft. I am also grateful to Rob and Liz Campling for providing me with accommodation on my many visits to the Emsworth area.

The Emsworth Maritime and Historical Trust has allowed me to reproduce a number of photographs from its collection and has given me access to its archive material. I am particularly grateful to the Trust's Administrator, Mrs Tessa Daines, for the help she has given. With her wide knowledge of Emsworth's history and her dedication to the cause of preserving the town's rich heritage, she has been an invaluable source of information and inspiration.

My thanks are due to the following for supplying photographs and illustrations (as numbered in the text): Chris Brunning (CJB Photography, Medina Road, Portsmouth) for the aerial photographs, 138, 145; Sir Edward Cazalet, 73; Michael Edwards, 131; Eileen Higham/ Emsworth Slipper Sailing Club, 55, 88, 103, 124, 125, 126, 130, 141, 142, 143, 144; Captain Peter Kimm, 120; Neil Michael Lodge, 1, 4, 5, 47; Barry Mapley, 15, 38, 43, 53, 59, 63, 65, 66, 76, 104, 105, 128; Vic Mitchell, 29, 30, 36, 37; Thelma Parham, 86, 87; John Reger, 6; Cathy Rudkin, 52, 54, 60, 62, 68, 71, 72, 82, 91, 107; Colin Urry, 58, 61, 64, 74, 75, 78, 92, 97, 127, 139; Vivian Williams, 98, 112, 117, 137; Tony Yoward, 16, 40, 42.

Introduction

Emsworth has a long and fascinating history. Passed by in Roman and Saxon times as unsuitable for settlement, the site was originally chosen as a new market place by Herbert Fitzherbert in 1239. Being in such close proximity to the sheltered waters of Chichester Harbour, it was inevitable that the new settlement would quickly develop into a community engaged in fishing and coastal trading. Boat building and milling soon followed as important local industries. By the 18th century Emsworth was the largest port in Chichester Harbour; it was also an important centre for milling, sail and ropemaking and the timber trade. The Emsworth oyster gained recognition far beyond the shores of the Harbour for its particularly fine flavour. In the 19th century Emsworth was a flourishing little town. Since the early 20th century, however, there has been a long and steady decline of local industries and the town has become more a place of residence than a place of work. It has also become an important centre for recreational sailing, once again taking advantage of the sheltered waters of Chichester Harbour. Emsworth, however, has not become a mere suburb of the larger town of Portsmouth to the west. It retains its separate identity and its unique character.

Much has already been written about Emsworth's history. John Reger, David Rudkin, Roy and Sheila Morgan and, more recently, Linda Newell, have all written about aspects of the town's past. As always with historical research, however, there is still a need for further research and revised interpretations. The aim of this book is to extend and develop our knowledge and to produce a detailed narrative of Emsworth's past.

I

The Medieval Origins of Emsworth

'A pair of gilt spurs'

The story of Emsworth begins in the early 13th century. Originally part of the manor of Warblington, Emsworth's origins can be traced to King John's decision to divide the manor in two at some date between 1204 and 1216, and to grant 100 shillings of land 'at Emelesworth' to William Aguillon for an annual rent of 'a pair of gilt spurs'. This grant was later confirmed by John's son, Henry III, in 1231. Legally the manor of Emsworth was a freeholding within the manor of Warblington, and the inhabitants of Emsworth still had to attend the manorial court at Warblington if they were seeking justice, but the separate existence of Emsworth had been established by these royal charters.

In April 1239 Henry III granted a further charter to Herbert Fitzherbert allowing a market to be held every Wednesday and an annual fair at 'Emelesworth in Warblington'. Medieval markets were spread quite evenly through the country, the distance between neighbouring markets averaging around three miles. This separation was considered necessary to prevent harmful competition between neighbouring markets. Since there was already a market at Havant, controlled by the monks of Winchester Cathedral, any charter for a new market would only be granted if it were sufficiently far away. Warblington village was too close but, at a distance of nearly two and a half miles, Emsworth was well placed as the site for the new market.

The area around Emsworth has yielded extensive evidence of settlement over a long period of time. A collection of worked flints – scrapers, blades, points and cores in glossy black flint – was found near Warblington in 1962. Flint tools have also been found within the boundaries of modern Emsworth. The Emsworth Museum has flint scrapers and other tools found at three locations – in Bath Road, in Victoria Road and in North Street. This indicates human activity, if not human settlement, in the area as early as the Neolithic period (around 3000 B.C.). During the Iron Age the area was settled by a Gaulish tribe, the Atrebates, who spread into south-eastern Hampshire from their landing site at Selsey. After the Roman Conquest an important town was established at Chichester (*Noviomagus Regnensium*) and an important port on the shore of Chichester Harbour at Fishbourne. The Romans also built a road along the coast from *Noviomagus Regnensium* to *Clausentum* (Bitterne). This road, which roughly followed the line of the present A259, passed through the site of modern Emsworth, but no Roman settlement appears to have been established there. There was, however, a substantial Roman villa at what is now Warblington. Archaeological remains reveal that the villa was built of brick and stone, with mosaic floors and possibly a hypocaust heating system. All of this indicates a high-status building. The discovery of a Roman kitchen midden at

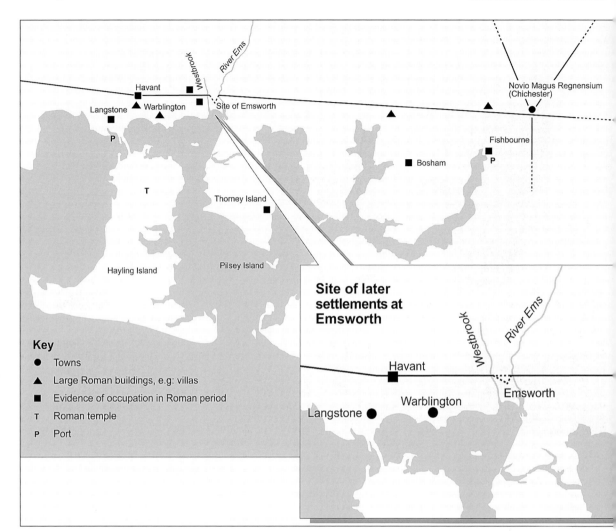

1 *Map showing known Roman settlements in the Chichester Harbour area. It has been assumed that the line of the road along the* ● *continued in an undeviating straight line through Emsworth. This would have roughly followed the route of the present A259 inner by* ● *road. When this road was built in the 1970s, however, no evidence of an earlier Roman road was found. It is possible that the road dev* ● *at this point to avoid low-lying, possibly marshy ground between the two tidal streams. The raised ground to the south of this line w* ● *have offered a drier route through the area. Without firm archaeological evidence, however, the line of the road through Emsworth must re* ● *a matter for conjecture. Two possible routes are shown on the map as dotted lines.*

49 Warblington Road in 1970 and of fragments of Roman roof tiles in the Selangor Avenue area both indicate the presence of Roman habitations on the western side of modern Emsworth. Roman artefacts have also been discovered on Thorney Island to the south of the town.

After the Romans departed in the early fifth century the area was settled by the Saxons. Around A.D. 500 they reoccupied the site of the Roman villa and established the village of *Weorblington*, the place of Weorbel's people. The site chosen was on good farmland, which was above the level of high tide but close enough to the shore to allow fishing in the harbour, and there was an adequate water supply from local springs. This is the site now occupied by

2 *A view of the church of St Thomas à Becket at Warblington. The earliest church building on this site was Saxon and was dedicated to 'Our Lady'. Much of the present church dates from the 13th century, and extensions were built in the 19th century, but part of the original Saxon church still remains, forming the central part of the tower.*

Warblington church and the remains of the castle. Warblington grew and flourished over the next five centuries. Christianity came to the area in the late seventh century and some time later the first church was built at Warblington. Viking raids on coastal settlements in the ninth century disturbed the peace of the area, although the main targets appear to have been Chichester and Bosham. By the time of the Norman Conquest in 1066 the manor of Warblington, together with the manors of Westbourne, Bosham and Fishbourne, was held by Harold Godwinson, Earl of Wessex and newly crowned King of England. After the Conquest William the Conqueror redistributed these lands, and in Domesday Book of 1086

Warblington is listed as being in the possession of Roger Montgomery, Earl of Shrewsbury. Of Emsworth, however, there is no mention at all.

Most of the features that made Warblington a good site for a settlement were also present at Emsworth. Fertile soil, a raised position and a sheltered anchorage for boats all combined in later years to give Emsworth a favourable situation. Crucially, however, the site of Emsworth lacked a good supply of drinking water. This is somewhat surprising in view of the fact that the centre of Emsworth is bounded on its eastern side by the River Ems and on its western side by the Westbrook. Both of these watercourses were, however, tidal, and this rendered the water

3 *An original Saxon window in the tower of the church of St Thomas à Becket.*

unsuitable for drinking. There were springs along the shoreline (at the foot of present-day South Street) but these were covered at high tide. Changes in climate in the 12th century led to a general fall in sea level and this would have uncovered the springs, thus making the site more habitable. It was probably this event which paved the way for the foundation of Emsworth in the 13th century.

That there was some Saxon occupation in the vicinity of Emsworth is shown by the discovery, in the 1960s, of 11th-century Saxon remains in the Seafields/Beacon Square area of the town. The finds included pottery shards, loom weights, oyster shells and animal bones; the archaeological excavation also uncovered evidence of a midden, a possible weaving shelter and an occupation floor, together with fragments of daub, a common building material. The remains of an iron bucket fitting were also unearthed. All of this suggests a small settlement, the inhabitants of which engaged in fishing, farming and the weaving of cloth. The Saxon origin of the name Emsworth – *Aemil's worth* – also indicates the existence of a Saxon settlement of some kind. A *worth* was an enclosed plot of land on which a house stood and Ems is a corruption of *Aemil's* or *Aemele's*, denoting the original ownership of this plot. We may surmise, therefore, that by the 11th century a Saxon farmstead had been established on the western side of the place now known as Emsworth.

Most new settlements in the Middle Ages resulted from decisions made by feudal lords.

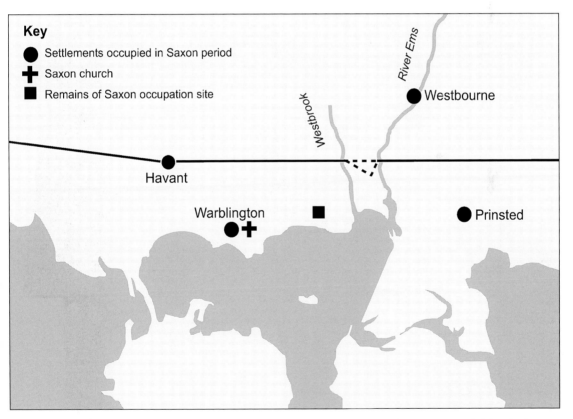

4 *Map showing Saxon settlement in the Emsworth area. The site of modern Emsworth was not yet settled, but the Saxon origin of the name, Aemil's worth, suggests some form of occupation on or near the site. The Roman road was still in use in the Saxon period.*

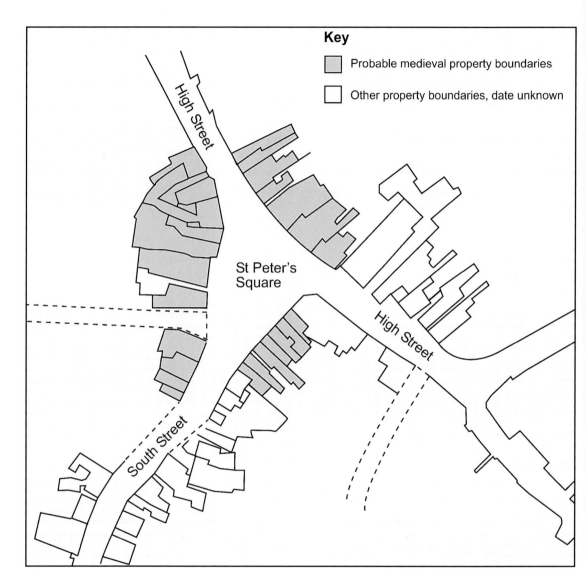

5 *Map of the modern centre of Emsworth showing the original road layout. The triangular St Peter's Square was the site of the medieval market place which provided the original reason for the village's foundation. Many of the property boundaries in the High Street and the Square show the typical medieval pattern of long, narrow plots stretching back from the street. The plots which have much broader frontages may have been formed by combining two plots together at some point in their history. The smaller plots may have been the sites of market stalls which, over a period of time, became more permanent structures.*

Emsworth fitted this pattern. It was a founded village that had been promoted by the lord of the manor, Matthew Fitzherbert, and was further developed by his son, Herbert. The plan of Emsworth exhibits many features that were characteristic of medieval foundations. The central, open market place (now St Peter's Square) was triangular in shape because it developed at a T-shaped road junction. South Street was the road leading down to the foreshore, where it is likely that some fishing was already being carried out. High Street was the main road through the settlement and was probably established along the line of the old Roman road. In order to maximise the use of space the houses and shops fronting the square and along High Street were built on long, narrow plots stretching back from the street. The frontages of these buildings would probably have been used for the selling of wares that had been made in the workshops behind. The long backyards would have been used for keeping animals, growing vegetables and storing tools and materials. A road led down to the harbour, where ships could load and unload. The Roman road along the coast was still in use in the Middle Ages and would have brought trade to the market. It is also likely that the line of North Street followed an older track that would have linked the coastal communities with inland settlements such as Westbourne. A study of modern maps of Emsworth shows that the road layout and property boundaries in the centre of the village still exhibit the basic pattern established in the Middle Ages.

In owing its existence to a royal charter giving the lord of the manor the right to hold a market and an annual fair, Emsworth already had some of the characteristics of a town. Ownership and control, however, remained in the hands of the feudal lord. The cost of obtaining the royal charter had to be recouped by the lord laying out tenements and charging rent for them. The original grant to William Aguillon allowed him to collect 100s. rent annually from certain villeins in Emsworth. The lord could also profit by charging rents on market stalls, by collecting tolls from outsiders who wished to use the market, and by imposing fines on those who breached the town's regulations. In many medieval communities that began in this way, growing prosperity enabled the townspeople to assert their independence by applying for a royal charter of their own, which would grant the town the right of self-government, and by building a wall around the town. Neither of these developments happened in Emsworth. The administration of justice was still controlled by the manorial court at Warblington. Emsworth remained a part of Warblington parish and its inhabitants had to travel to Warblington for weekly worship and for baptisms, marriages and burials. In these respects Emsworth had little more status than a hamlet.

The separation of the manors of Warblington and Emsworth was not without its problems. In 1312 Isabel Aguillon, who had inherited the manor, sued Robert le Ewer, lord of the manor of Warblington, for trespass on her lands at Emsworth. The following year she appealed to the king for the restitution of her lands which had been seized on an inquisition into her rights. It was then stated that the original grant to Robert Aguillon had referred only to the right to collect rents in Emsworth, but that he had usurped the lordship of the villeins and a fishery in Emsworth. How this dispute was resolved is not recorded.

The evidence suggests that Emsworth experienced growing prosperity and importance during the Middle Ages. Documentary evidence from this time is very fragmentary but the frequent references to Emsworth in the Court and Patent Rolls suggest that it became an important creek within the Port of Chichester during the 13th and 14th centuries. In 1341 Emsworth was one of five ports in Hampshire that were ordered to provide ships to carry the new Keeper of the Channel Islands to his post. In 1343 the lordship of the submanor of Emsworth was purchased by Nicholas Devenish, who was an important wool merchant and who at one time had been mayor of Winchester. Wool was one of the principal exports from the Port of Chichester and it is likely that under Devenish's control the little port of Emsworth would have participated in this trade. Evidence of an import trade in wine through Emsworth comes from the appointment in 1346 of Richard Marshall as a 'gauger of wines' at a number of south-coast ports, including Emsworth. There is also some evidence of illicit trade through the port: in 1378 a special commission was appointed to investigate the smuggling of goods to France from Emsworth.

As well as seaborne trade, fishing also became important to the local economy. In 1340, at the death of the lord of the manor of Warblington, Thomas Monthermer, an inquest was held into the value of his estate. From this we learn that the Emsworth fishery was valued at 6s. 8d., a not inconsiderable sum at that time.

However, with the arrival of the Black Death in 1348 the slow but steady growth of Emsworth was temporarily halted. No specific evidence exists for the effects of the plague on Emsworth, but it is known that the disease hit nearby communities severely. The Isle of Wight was virtually depopulated. Calculations of the population of Apuldram show a 35 per cent decline in population during the 14th century. Emsworth would not have escaped this national disaster and we can assume that the decline in population was at least close to the national average of around 40 per cent in both Emsworth and Warblington. It would be several generations before the population could recover from the devastation of the Black Death. Meanwhile, during the 15th century, the manor of Warblington came into the possession of the powerful Neville family. Richard Neville, Earl of Warwick, turned the fields around Warblington castle and church into a deer park. The farmers, many of whose families had occupied this land for generations, were turned out and relocated in the north of the manor. Warblington virtually ceased to exist as a village and the centre of gravity of the manor, both in population and in economic terms, shifted even more decisively towards Emsworth.

II

1500–1720

'Two hundred large pirl oysters'

The upheavals in Church and State that occurred during the 16th and 17th centuries had a direct impact on Warblington. The inhabitants of Emsworth were less directly involved but their lives were nevertheless affected by the Reformation of the Church and by the political struggles of the 1640s.

During the reign of Henry VIII the manor of Warblington was granted to Margaret, Countess of Salisbury. She decided to make Warblington her principal residence and in 1515 she gave orders for the construction of a large castle on the site of the old manor house. Built around four sides of a square, with a large central courtyard within and towers at each of the four corners, the castle was indeed an imposing building. A fortified gatehouse with towers on either side guarded the entrance to the building, but in other respects the castle was designed for spacious and comfortable living. In the 17th century it was described thus:

> a very fair place, well moated about, built all of bricks and stones … with a fair green court within and the buildings around the said court, with a fair gallery and divers chambers of great count.

The finished castle was grand enough to entertain royalty and the king duly obliged by visiting Warblington, together with his daughter Mary, in 1526.

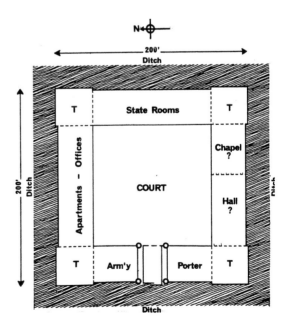

6 *An artist's impression of 16th-century Warblington Castle, looking towards the main gateway. This imposing building was largely the work of Margaret, Countess of Salisbury.*

9

Margaret fell out of favour with Henry VIII in the 1530s. Already viewed with suspicion because of her close links with the House of York, her decision to defy the king and retain her Catholic faith during the Reformation of the 1530s sealed her fate. She was accused of treason and, by 1540, was executed.

The manor reverted to royal ownership until, in 1552, it was given by Edward VI to one of his courtiers, Sir Richard Cotton, who dutifully put his castle at the young king's disposal in the same year 'on his journey to the sea coast for the recovery of his health'. Even the bracing sea air of Warblington, however, could not restore the young and sickly king to health; he died the following year. The next lord of the manor, Sir George Cotton, converted to Catholicism in the 1570s during the reign of Elizabeth I and Warblington became a centre of Catholic resistance on the south coast for the next 40 years. A list of Hampshire 'recusants' from 1577 included a Mrs Edborow Bullaker, who was said to have harboured Catholic priests in her house at Warblington. In 1582 a priest, John Chapman, admitted he had made the Bullaker house his chief abode. In the late 1590s there were said to have been 19 recusants at Warblington, more than in any other village in the area.

The position of Warblington on the coast heightened the concerns of the authorities about the Catholic sympathies of many local families. In 1576 two boys, John Cotton and Robert Southwell, left Warblington by ship to travel to school and exile in France. This was one of many similar journeys made during the reign of Elizabeth I between the harbours and creeks of Hampshire and Sussex and the French coast. For incoming Catholic priests there were advantages in making a landing at or near Warblington, where there were many sympathetic local families who would be willing to hide them from the authorities. Since Emsworth was the nearest port to Warblington it is very likely that many of these journeys were made in vessels from Emsworth.

7 In 1576 Robert Southwell, together with John Cotton, left Warblington by sea to travel to school and exile in France. After a Jesuit education in Douai, he was ordained a Catholic priest in 1584 and returned to England in 1586 to conduct secret missionary work. He was provided with a safe house in London by his friend John Cotton. He was arrested in 1592 and executed in 1595.

8 All that remains of Warblington Castle after it was 'slighted' in the Civil War is this single turret, part of the original gateway.

The Cotton family paid a heavy price for their Catholicism. In the 1580s Sir George Cotton was ordered to pay fines of £260 p.a. for his crime of being a recusant, an enormous sum at that time. He was later imprisoned, and when he died in 1609 his body was ordered to be buried in an open field. Even this did not break the resistance of the Cottons for, in the same year, it was reported that 'in the house of Mr Cotton of Hampshire there is harboured a Jesuit who

9 *Speed's map of Hampshire, 1611. Emsworth is shown as 'Einsworth', reflecting the fact that there were a number of different versions of the name before the modern spelling was adopted as standard. The placing of Einsworth some distance to the north of its true position, and the inaccuracy in drawing the line of the River Ems, show that surveying was still very much in its infancy. (Hampshire Record Office Ref. 139M89)*

names himself Thomas Singleton. He teaches the grandchildren of the said Cotton.'

In the Civil War of the 1640s the Cottons supported the Crown against Parliament. In 1643 the castle was besieged by Parliamentary forces and after it was captured it was 'slighted'. All that remained was one of the gatehouse towers, which

was subsequently used as a dovecote. Following the destruction of the castle the building materials were dispersed around the district and some of the valuable dressed stone found its way into houses in Emsworth. The Cotton family remained as lords of the manors of Warblington and Emsworth until the family line died out in 1736. The feudal

10 *A modern picture of the Town Mill in Queen Street. Records suggest that there has been a mill on this site since at least the 16th century.*

power of the lord of the manor, however, had been severely weakened, although not destroyed, by these events.

What of the inhabitants of Emsworth during these turbulent times? It is likely that the fishing, farming and trading folk of Emsworth were more concerned with the immediate priorities of earning a living than with the struggles in Church and State, although they would have witnessed the events at Warblington at close quarters and, since religion was central to the lives of people of all classes, the conflicts of the 16th and 17th centuries would have had an impact on their lives.

Some indication as to the size of the population of Emsworth can be gleaned from the militia reckonings of the 16th century. In 1544, during a war against France, there was a French landing on the Isle of Wight and the Hampshire militia were sent to the relief of the island. Emsworth and Portchester together sent a total of 270 men. In the 1574 militia reckoning for Bosmere Hundred, however, Warblington and Emsworth could produce only 45 able-bodied men. Reger has extrapolated from this that the number of heads of families in Warblington and Emsworth at this time was between fifty and sixty. This would translate into a population of between 220 and 240 for the whole parish, based on an average of four persons per household.

In 1664-5 the people of the county were assessed for payment of the Hearth Tax. This was a tax, granted by Parliament to Charles II, which was levied on every householder who paid the poor rate, and was based on the number of hearths in each property. In Emsworth the tax was paid by 31 householders, with another 21 householders excused. In the whole parish of Warblington a total of 56 households were liable for the tax and 35 excused. This would translate into a total population for the whole parish of around 400, of whom a little over 200 would have lived in Emsworth. It seems clear, therefore, that the population had roughly doubled in the century following the reign of Queen Elizabeth I.

Earning a living in Emsworth was based for many on the traditional occupation of fishing. A 1503 manorial court record mentions a mullet fishery in the manor. When John Holloway, a fisherman, died in 1559 he left his son 'half the little boat'. The inventory of his goods and chattels recorded two boats and various farm animals, indicating not only that he was one of the more substantial fishermen of the town but also that not all of his income was derived from fishing. The will of Philip Hewitt of Emsworth, dated 1596, showed that he owned a 'half-share in a boat or dredge' worth 20 shillings and 'a fishing nett'. In 1671 William Spriggs of Emsworth died owning a hoy (a type of small fishing boat) and two other small boats, along with fishing tackle such as nets and drags. The references to dredges and drags is an indication of involvement in oyster fishing. The importance of oysters to the local economy is confirmed by a 1688 source in which two men agreed to pay their manorial lord '200 large pirl oysters' annually on the Friday following the feast of All Saints for the rental of oyster ponds in the harbour. In the previous year John Holloway had been fined one shilling by the manorial court 'for digging coaves in his lordship's fishing'. For some Emsworth inhabitants, such as John Manser and Richard Hedger, fishing appears to have been a full-time occupation and one that could provide a comfortable living. At his death in 1673 John Manser owned goods and chattels to the value of £8 13s. 4d. together with his house, outbuildings and an area of land. Other Emsworth men seemed to have combined fishing with other occupations

such as farming. For example, in 1677 Edward Rowlands owned a boat together with 'three acres of corn in the common field', once again indicating that fishermen could also be farmers. Both of these men had, in their different ways, been able to make a substantial living.

By the 17th century other trades and industries were beginning to be established in Emsworth. It is likely that the fishing boats used by local fishermen were made in the town. The existence of a boat-building and shipbuilding industry in Emsworth in the 17th century is confirmed by the probate records. John Hewitt, who died in 1607, and Isaac Hatch, who died in 1618, were both described as shipwrights. The inventory of the property of John Smith, who died in 1700, lists a boat-building yard on the Westbrook and two vessels under construction. Associated with shipbuilding were related trades such as ropemaking. Christopher Richard, who died in 1719, owned a ropewalk at the Hermitage on the Sussex side of the River Ems.

Milling had been established in Emsworth at least as early as the 16th century. The earliest reference to a mill in Emsworth is in 1570, when Thomas Swyft the miller died. By 1632 the Town Mill, on the site of the present day Queen Street mill, had developed into a combined wheat mill and malt mill under the same roof and it was let at a rent of £20. There is also evidence of the manufacture of clay pipes for tobacco smoking, and a possible link to the Taplin family of Chichester, who were the main pipe-makers in the area. Seaborne trade was also important. In 1714 Thomas Hendy, originally from Havant but married into the Manser family of Emsworth, was described as the master of a trading vessel that carried grain from Emsworth to Chichester. At this time the main outward-bound cargo of ships trading from Emsworth was unmilled grain. Inward cargoes included coal, probably from north-eastern ports. In 1663 John Wheeler of Emsworth gave a piece of land called the 'coal yard mead' to his daughter. In 1684 Daniel

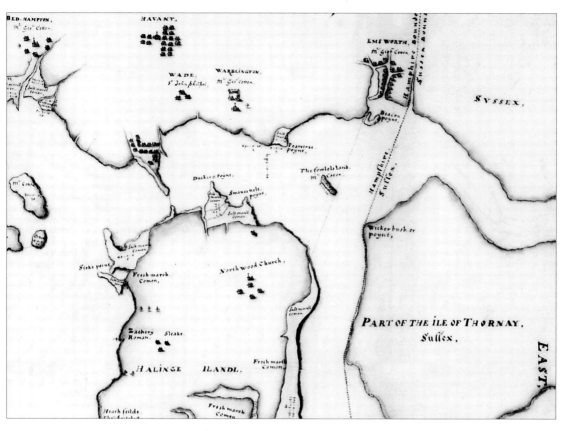

11 *La Favelure's map of the Portsea area, drawn in 1665, is more accurate than the earlier map by Speed. The street pattern is shown for the first time and the map shows buildings along the length of South Street, the Square and High Street. The map also records that the ownership of the manor of Emsworth is in the hands of Mr George Cotton. (British Library, MS 1 6371 A)*

Wheeler died, leaving 40 tons of coal among his goods and chattels. He also owned a vessel worth £80.

For a community dependent on commerce, access to wider markets was the key to prosperity. As we have seen, Emsworth was beginning to establish itself as an important port within Chichester Harbour and its merchants were engaged in coastal trade with neighbouring towns. Road communications were also important if a port was to be able to serve its hinterland. Here the picture was not so rosy. The old Roman road along the south coast was still the main arterial route, but this had long since fallen into a state of disrepair. The court rolls of the manor show

that efforts were made to keep the road clear and in a good state of repair. John Smyth was taken to task in 1628 for having 'encroached upon the highway in Emsworth … and he is commanded to level the incroachment … before the feast of All Saints next, under the penalty of 10s.'. In 1632 the inhabitants of Emsworth were ordered not to 'place any sea ore in the street of Emsworth'. In 1687 the manorial court ordered that 'the inhabitants and land occupiers of Emsworth [must] sufficiently cleave stone and gravel the streets' in order that 'the king's liege people may at all times pass through dry shod'. This had to be done before Lady Day, 'on pain of twenty shillings'. It was the inhabitants who

12 *This pharmacy at 38 High Street occupied the oldest surviving building in Emsworth, which dates from the 17th century. Since this photograph was taken the pharmacy has moved to new premises.*

this bridge was first built is unclear. A map of 1665 shows no bridge here but it does appear on a map of 1724. Even though the bridge would have been under water at exceptionally high tides it was undoubtedly better than the old causeway that had previously been the only means of crossing the river at this point.

The manorial court, consisting of the representatives of the lord of the manor and the tenants, still had responsibility in the first instance for law and order within the village. The repair and maintenance of any instruments of punishment in Emsworth were the responsibility of the inhabitants. In 1620 it was reported to the court that the whipping post was 'in ruin'. Three years later the court heard that 'the stocks within the tything of Emsworth are out of repair', and it commanded the inhabitants to repair them. When it was reported at the next meeting that the stocks had not been repaired, they were fined a sum of 6s. 8d. Bakers who cheated their customers by selling underweight loaves were fined on two occasions, whilst the wife of John Smyth was denounced as 'a common scold' and was sentenced to 'punishment by the tumbrel'.

Emsworth was becoming a more prosperous and substantial community by the end of the 17th century. This impression is confirmed by reference to the buildings in the town. On a map of 1665 showing Emsworth and the harbour, drawn by La Favelure, all the houses in Emsworth were around the Square or in South Street. This was much the same area as had been occupied by the original settlement in the Middle Ages, although there would undoubtedly have been more dwellings by the mid-17th century. Since the oldest surviving buildings in modern Emsworth date from the 17th century, it seems that this was a time when some of the more prosperous residents were beginning to invest in more substantial brick or stone properties to replace the timber-framed buildings that had been constructed in the Middle Ages. The oldest surviving building is at 38 High Street, a property that has been

were blamed for the state of the roads passing through Emsworth and the onus was placed on them to make the necessary improvements. The court's injunction, however, appears to have been ignored, for at a subsequent meeting of the manorial court in 1688 the order was repeated. The manorial court had also ordered, in 1686, 'all person that lay down dung or soil in the street to remove the same on pain of five shillings on default'.

None of these orders and threats seems to have had much effect, for in the mid-18th century the coast road was still a narrow, pot-holed and hazardous route. Some improvement in road communications was made through the construction of a bridge over the River Ems between Emsworth and the Hermitage. When

used as a pharmacy since the early 19th century. There are also some 17th-century survivals in the buildings along South Street.

Growing prosperity was not, however, the experience of every inhabitant of Emsworth at this time. During the 1630s the efforts of Sir John Oglander to collect Ship Money for Charles I from the towns along this coast were not very successful. More than half of those liable to pay this tax were defaulters and, while this may reflect resistance to paying this highly unpopular tax itself, the pleas of the people of the area tell a different story:

> Owr monyes riseth far more heavier and therefore harder to be gathered than that of Sussex. For from Emsworth to Christchurch all along the sea coasts beinge thirty miles in length the inhabitants (most fischermen) are so poore as they are not able to paye and most of them have not whereon to distrayne.

The Hearth Tax record also tells a similar story. Of the 52 households in Emsworth, 31 were assessed as being liable to pay the tax. Of these, six houses had only one hearth, 18 had two and six had three hearths. Only one house, that belonging to William Pragnell, was large enough to accommodate five hearths. No Emsworth house was as large as the Parsonage in Warblington which had seven hearths, or as grand as the houses of Mr Boxhill in Warblington and Mr Hyde in Newtimber, which had 10 hearths each. Of the 21 Emsworth houses which were excused paying the tax, all but three of them had only one hearth each. These figures reveal that the majority of Emsworth houses at this time were comparatively small and that many of the inhabitants were relatively poor. On the other hand, the wide disparities in wealth that were evident in more rural communities such as Warblington, between the landowning gentry and the labouring poor, were not as apparent

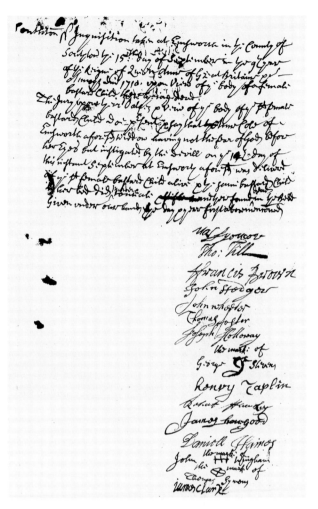

13 *This record of an inquest (inquisition) held at Emsworth in 1710 into the death of a 'female bastard child' is a rare survival from the early 18th century. The jury of 15 men found that 'Johanna Cole of Emsworth aforesaid widdow having not the fear of God before her but instigated by the devill on the 12th day of … September at Emsworth … was delivered of ye said female bastard child alive and ye same bastard child did murder to which [was] found dead in ye bedd'. The document was signed by some of Emsworth's leading citizens of the time, including Thomas Till, John Hedger, Joseph Holloway and Henry Taplin, although not all of the jury were able to sign their own names. The document gives an interesting insight into the attitudes of the period. (Hampshire Record Office 202M85/4/14/19)*

in Emsworth. We may conclude, then, that the community would have been relatively close-knit and self-sufficient.

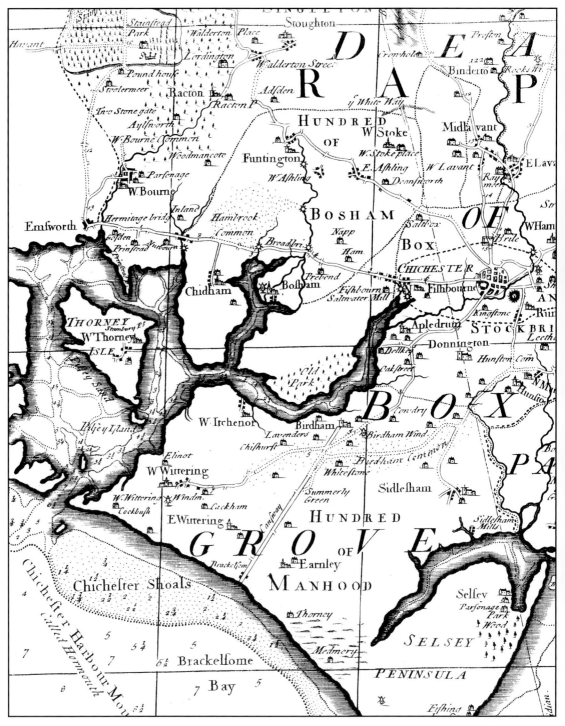

14 *Richard Budgen's map, 1724. Although primarily a map of Sussex, this does show the road pattern around Emsworth with a reasonable degree of accuracy. Some buildings are marked along the High Street and the Square. On the Sussex side of the border several mills are marked around Chichester Harbour, but none of the Emsworth mills has been included. (West Sussex Record Office)*

III

1720–1790

'They grind and dress the corn'

During the course of the 18th century the small port of Emsworth grew to become the largest port in Chichester Harbour. The milling industry expanded and the town's quays were increasingly busy handling the loading of corn, milled flour and timber and the unloading of coal. The fishing industry grew in importance and a new shipyard, built at the end of Sweare Lane (later King Street), began the construction of much larger vessels than had been previously possible. The High Street and St Peter's Square became an important local centre for trade and commerce. The small village, which had originated as a venue for a weekly market and an annual fair and had grown up in

the shadow of the more established community of Warblington, was developing into a small but thriving town in its own right.

Much of the prosperity of 18th-century Emsworth can be attributed to the commercial success of the town's corn mills. In 1720 there was one water mill in Emsworth: the Town Mill (or Lord's Mill) in Queen Street, set alongside a branch of the River Ems. It was clearly a substantial mill even at that early date for it was described by Defoe as being 'two mills under one roof'. In other words, both wheat and malt were milled there. By 1790, there were two mills in Emsworth itself and another two nearby on the Sussex side

15 *The Quay Mill. This late 19th-century photograph shows a sizeable complex of buildings, including the mill itself, a grain store to the right and the miller's house.*

16 *Lumley Mill. This late 19th-century photograph shows an extensive range of buildings from different stages in the mill's history. The hipped roofs are a common feature of 18th- and 19th-century buildings in this area.*

of the River Ems. In addition to the Town Mill, Emsworth had acquired Quay Mill some time around the middle of the 18th century. This new mill, built on the harbour side near the foot of South Street (at that time known as Saffron Hill), was a tidal mill and its construction would have involved considerable financial investment. The lower reaches of the Westbrook were dammed by the construction of an enclosing wall in order to create a millpond. Incoming tidal water entered the millpond through sluice gates and was then trapped, to be released through the mill race at a steady flow to drive the mill machinery. The waters of the Westbrook were also harnessed to drive the mill when the tidal waters had been exhausted, thereby ensuring that the mill could be kept in operation for longer.

On the Sussex side of the River Ems there were mills at Lumley and the Hermitage. The Hermitage, or Slipper Mill, was also a tidal mill and appears to have been built earlier than the Quay Mill, perhaps as early as the 1730s. It was owned by Thomas Hendy, who also owned the Town Mill. Hendy enlarged the millpond and the mill itself, and built a wharf for the corn barges known as Hendy's Quay. Lumley Mill, also built around the middle of the 18th century, was a water mill powered by the waters of the River Ems. It was built by Lord Lumley.

The reasons for this change in Emsworth's fortunes are not hard to find. Situated as it was at the heart of a highly fertile agricultural area, the town was well placed to benefit from the growing demand for food resulting from an expanding population. Two markets in particular were of special interest to Emsworth's millers and merchants. The nearby naval town of Portsmouth grew in size and importance during the 18th

17 *Isaac Taylor's one-inch map of Hampshire, 1759. Taylor has shown both Lumley Mill and the Town Mill in the Emsworth area. Emsworth Common, to the north of the village, is shown as a largely wooded area. King Street and Tower Lane are marked on the map, although Tower Lane is shown as branching off King Street. The seaside millpond on the western side of Emsworth and the Slipper millpond on the eastern side have not yet appeared on a map. (Hampshire Record Office Ref. 139M89)*

century as a consequence of the frequent wars against France. Navy contracts to supply food for the ships' crews (and indeed timber products for the ships themselves) were a spur to agriculture, industry and commerce in the surrounding area. The rapid expansion of the London market, however, was of far greater importance to Emsworth's success. In the 17th century farmers and corn merchants in Hampshire, Sussex and Surrey had sold unmilled grain destined for London through Farnham market in Surrey. This trade involved long and expensive transport by road. From the 1730s London's needs were supplied in a more cost-effective way that involved the milling of the grain near its point of origin and the transport of milled flour (or meal) by sea to London. Daniel Defoe, in his *Tour through the Whole Island of Great Britain*, written in 1742, described the changes thus:

> Some money'd men of Chichester, Emsworth and other places adjacent, joined their stocks together, and built large granaries near the Crook, where the vessels came up; and here they buy and lay up all the corn which the country on that side can spare and having good mills in the neighbourhood, they grind and dress the corn and send it to London in the meal … by long sea.

He went on to say that 'this carrying of meal by sea is now practised from several other places on this coast, even as far as Southampton'. The expansion of the milling industry in the Emsworth area in the second half of the 18th century was a direct consequence of the growing demand for food from the London market and the changing ways of meeting that demand.

Landowners and farmers played their part in boosting the yields of farms in the area and creating the surplus of corn that was available to supply the London market. The fertility of the brickearth soil of the coastal plain was enhanced by changes in agricultural methods

– part of the widespread agricultural revolution that was occurring at the time. An important part of this change was the enclosure movement, through which the great open fields of medieval Hampshire were being replaced by more compact farms with enclosed fields. By the mid-18th century this process was already well advanced in south Hampshire. Warblington Farm, Castle Farm, Emsworth (Coldharbour) Farm and Mayze Coppice Farm had been enclosed by the 1750s. There still remained, however, two open fields, the Highland Field and the Sea Field, and a large common field of some 700 acres in area. In 1810 the common was enclosed by private Act of Parliament. The lion's share of this land was taken by the lord of the manor, with much of the rest being divided among about thirty families who held copyholds in the manor. The Act of Parliament gave some protection to the common rights of the rest of the population by stipulating that 'a portion of the common called Coldharbour Green' should be given 'as and for a place of amusement for the inhabitants of the said parish forever'. The remaining open fields were enclosed and divided by another Act of Parliament in 1820. Once the land had been enclosed the local farmers were free to introduce new crops and machinery that increased the yields of their farms.

Taking the 'long sea' route to London was undoubtedly much further than going by road but, given the state of the roads in the first half of the 18th century, sea transport was cheaper and more reliable, especially for the transport of bulky cargoes such as corn meal and malt. The development of sea trade in milled grain pulled the centre of gravity of the milling industry towards the coast. Emsworth was not alone in benefiting from the expansion of milling and the growing coastal trade. All along the shores of Chichester Harbour, from Birdham and Dell Quay in the east, through Fishbourne, Bosham, Nutbourne, Emsworth, Warblington and on to Hayling and Langstone in the west, millers and merchants

18 *The site of John King's shipyard. Established in the mid-18th century by George Norris and John King, the yard was situated in what was then known as Sweare Lane (later King Street). After two centuries of shipbuilding on the site the yard closed, and the land has since been used for a housing development.*

rode the boom. But Emsworth was particularly well placed to take full advantage of the new opportunities. With the River Ems on one side and the Westbrook on the other there was an unusually favourable capacity for the development of water mills. There were also relatively narrow tidal channels where the waters could be trapped in millponds for driving tidal mills. The foresight of Emsworth merchants such as Thomas Hendy in investing in mills, tidal mill-ponds and quays was another factor. The fact that Emsworth's quays were owned by the merchants, unlike at Bosham, for example, where they were owned by the lord of the manor, meant that no harbour dues had to be paid on ships berthing in Emsworth. This gave Emsworth merchants a cost advantage over their rivals in other ports around the harbour.

With these advantages Emsworth became, during the course of the 18th century, the largest port in Chichester Harbour. There was a high level of activity on the quays of Emsworth from the mid-18th century through to the mid-19th century. Daly has calculated that in the year 1789-90 187 vessels, with an average displacement of 69 tons, entered and cleared the

port of Emsworth. Coal became an increasingly important commodity that was 'imported' through Emsworth. The coal yard referred to in the 1663 Court Book was again mentioned in 1749 when the Court Book referred to 'all those three quarters of an acre of land lying in a field called the cole yard, having a cole yard on the east part thereof'.

At this stage the coal yard was in the possession of Joseph Holloway, son of John Holloway, a mariner. Outgoing cargoes consisted mainly of milled flour but there was trade in other commodities as well. Between 1754 and 1758, 11,000 tons of malt were exported from Chichester Harbour, of which perhaps 40 per cent was loaded in Emsworth. Timber and timber products, particularly those required by the Royal Navy, were despatched from Emsworth to Portsmouth and, occasionally, to Plymouth. After 1730 a growing outward trade in woollen fleeces developed from Chichester, and Emsworth merchants later gained a share in this trade.

Not all of the outbound cargoes were destined for British ports since Emsworth merchants were also involved in the export trade. Here again they had an advantage over other, smaller, ports within Chichester Harbour. A charter granted by James II to Chichester in the 1680s had defined the limits of the Port of Chichester and decreed that Dell Quay was the only harbour within the port where foreign cargoes could be loaded. Although Emsworth was situated within Chichester Harbour it was not within the boundaries of the Port of Chichester and therefore escaped the restrictions placed on other ports such as Bosham. Ships loaded in Emsworth traded as far afield as Ireland, Holland, France, Spain and Portugal. The cargo of the vessel *Prosperous*, which sailed to Cork in 1731, illustrates the range of goods which were exported through Emsworth: '84 sacks containing 42 quarters of wheat, 112 quarters, 6 bushels of Dills in loose bags, 103 sacks containing 64 quarters, 3 bushels of wheat flour, Winchester measure'.

Some of the trade passing through Emsworth, particularly in the first half of the 18th century, was illicit. Silk, tobacco, tea, brandy and wine were smuggled through the small ports along this coast, and some houses were specially adapted for this purpose, with cellars and passages for the storage of goods. The inlets and creeks of Chichester Harbour were ideal locations for smugglers to unload their contraband goods and hand them over to the country people who largely controlled the trade. James Hunt, the landlord of the *Pack Horse* at Stansted, was implicated in smuggling in 1792. Emsworth has been listed as one of the major local centres for smuggling, together with Langstone, Farlington and Rowland's Castle. Customs officers had been stationed in Emsworth since 1671, at which time the post was held by John Hedger. In 1750 there was one Customs Riding officer based in Emsworth, although the records do not reveal his name, and by the late 18th century the local customs establishment was equipped with a revenue cutter, the *Swallow*. Despite the efforts of the customs officers, and the occasional support given to them by ships of the Royal Navy, smuggling continued throughout this

period. Indeed, once the long war with France began in 1793 and the Navy could no longer spare ships for assisting the revenue, the pace of smuggling activity increased.

The increase in seaborne trade led to an increased demand for ships. Emsworth was again well placed to respond to this growing demand with its long tradition of boat and shipbuilding. The original shipyard was on the Westbrook and was owned by the Smith family. When the tidal millpond was created for the new Quay Mill in the mid-18th century a new shipyard site was needed, and this was found at Sweare Lane on the other side of the town. The ownership of the shipyard also changed as the new yard came under the aegis of Norris and King. George Norris, who appears to have supplied the practical knowledge in the partnership, was the nephew of the rector of Warblington, the Rev. William Norris. His partner, John King, probably the business brain behind the partnership, was the son of Joseph King of Warblington. Originally from Titchfield, Joseph King was a landowner and farmer who owned substantial lands in Warblington, Titchfield, Warsash and Swanwick. John King and George Norris built the Emsworth shipyard into a successful and thriving business. The yard had two slipways and was capable of building vessels of up to 250 tons. The French wars brought unparalleled opportunities for a shipbuilding business so close to the large naval port of Portsmouth. Although the Navy constructed its own warships in the Portsmouth dockyard, the Emsworth yard of Norris and King supplied ships' boats and launches, boathooks, pike staves and capstan bars.

The main work of the yard, however, was the building of the coastal trading vessels of the kind that plied their trade through Emsworth. Between 1766 and 1789, 19 vessels were launched from this yard, 15 of which were built in the 1780s alone. Indeed, in 1788-9 the yard was exceptionally busy with no fewer than seven vessels being launched. Vessels such as the 183-ton brig *Polly,* launched in 1783, and the 131-ton brig *Commerce,* 1789, were built for the growing coal trade between the north-east ports and the south coast. There was also one schooner, the 67-ton *William* launched in 1788, and a number of smaller sloops which ranged in size from 25 tons to 60 tons. These smaller vessels were built for the coastal trade in grain and flour.

Fishing remained a mainstay of the local economy. In 1755, of 115 persons whose names and occupations were recorded, 19 were fishermen. A further 15 called themselves master mariners. Oyster fishing provided perhaps the most profitable catches. In 1788 it is recorded that 12 master fishermen dredged from the harbour a total of 7,035 bushels of oysters, worth over £1,500. The harbour, and the English Channel beyond, also had an abundance of other fish and shellfish to interest the local fishermen. Other shellfish which were landed were cockles, mussels

and winkles. Plaice, sole, flounder, whiting and grey mullet could be caught within the harbour whilst there were seasonal catches of mackerel and herring in the Channel.

Although transport by sea was vital to the local economy, travel by road was also important. Timber for the local shipyards and grain from local farms destined for the mills needed to be brought into Emsworth by road. Emsworth people needed to travel to Portsmouth and Chichester and, occasionally perhaps, to the more distant markets such as London on business trips. The poor state of the roads in the 18th century was therefore of concern to the townspeople. It was stated at the Hampshire Quarter Sessions in 1751 that the coast road was 'ruinous and impassable' at Bedhampton and for much of its route the road was little more than a single track and rutted lane. Exceptionally high tides or periods of prolonged rain caused flooding at the mouths of rivers such as the Ems and the Westbrook, making the coast road impassable. A stage wagon plying between Portsmouth and Chichester in the 1750s would take a whole day to complete the 18-mile journey. Improvements to the road came about as a result of the creation of the Cosham to Chichester Turnpike Trust in 1762. Under the 1762 Act of Parliament the Turnpike Trust was allowed to collect tolls from users of the road to pay for improvements and repairs. Toll gates were set up at Cosham, Bedhampton, Nutbourne, Fishbourne and Chichester to collect tolls, which varied from one shilling for a coach with six horses to three pence for a one-horse carriage.

In the wake of improvements to the main coast road regular coach services were established linking Portsmouth, Chichester and Brighton. Situated on the High Street, inns such as the *Crown* became coaching inns, providing food, refreshment and fresh horses for travellers. Emsworth's many inns already had an important role in local society. By the late 18th century there were at least six inns in the town. The *Crown* and the *Ship* in the

19   *St Peter's Chapel. This artist's impression shows the chapel as it would have looked when it was opened in 1789.*

High Street were the oldest, having been founded during the 17th century. To these were added the *Black Dog* (1711), the *Golden Lion* (1718), the *White Hart* (1718) and the *Sloop* (1795). Inns were not merely the focus of the social lives of many of Emsworth's residents, but also provided a meeting point for business dealings and a venue for the town's traditional and newly established institutions. The meetings of the manorial Court Baron, for example, were usually held in the *Crown Inn*. An Emsworth Friendly Society, established in 1763, was based at the *Black Dog Inn*.

Whilst the inns catered for many of the worldly needs of Emsworth's inhabitants, the spiritual needs of the majority were still met by the parish church at nearby Warblington. There was no nonconformist chapel in Emsworth during the 18th century, although there is a reference in *Micah Clarke* by Conan Doyle to services being held there towards the end of the 17th century:

> I was born in the year 1664 in the little village of Havant. As to the Independents, of whom my father was one, they were under the ban of the law, but they attended Conventicle at Emsworth whither we would trudge, rain or shine, on every Sabbath morning.

Roman Catholicism had, by the early part of the century, been reduced to the creed of a small minority. Despite their small numbers, however, the existence of Catholics within the parish so exercised the mind of the Reverend Mr Bradstone in 1727 that he wrote to the Bishop of Winchester about his concerns.

> I think myself obliged in duty to acquaint your Lordship of a late scandalous conversion of a woman and, I fear, her husband to the errors and corruptions of the Romish Church. This woman is the wife of one Thomas Wheeler, a shopkeeper, who constantly till lately came to church with her husband.

20 *The sale of a pew in St Peter's Chapel, 1828. Most of the pews or seats in the chapel were privately owned and could be bought and sold as a form of property. (Portsmouth City Record Office)*

He went on to assert that 'papists in this parish [are] persons of indifferent circumstance, only renters of two small farms', but he singled out one character for particular condemnation: 'There is a Papist in my Parish who keeps a publick house, a most impudent, audacious fellow and who I fear doth a great deal of mischief by travelling about.'

According to Bradstone local Catholics met for worship in 'a little poor house' in Havant, where there was a 'person who goes under the character of a priest', and they had the patronage of Lord Dormer, 'our bitter enemy'. In their efforts at conversion he claimed that the Catholics had been 'but too successful among the poorer sort especially, for generally speaking they prey upon none but the miserably necessitous and the wretchedly ignorant'.

Bradstone's alarmist tone reflected the intolerance that had been characteristic of the 17th century. Despite the continuing hostility to their presence, Catholics in the parish were able to establish a small chapel in Bedhampton and maintain a presence within the local community, and by the end of the 18th century a more tolerant approach in matters of religion was becoming evident.

A more pressing concern for the Anglican communicants of Emsworth was the fact that their place of worship, and the centre for the administration of parish affairs, was some distance from the town in Warblington. Attendance at church services on Sundays involved a journey of about one mile by road, or the shorter trek on foot along the seashore via the Church Path. In the 1780s a group of Emsworth's more substantial residents banded together to buy land in the Square and pay the costs for the construction of a new chapel. St Peter's Chapel was opened there in 1789. St Peter's Proprietary Chapel, so-called because it was owned by a group of shareholders, provided a place of worship for up to 500 souls. Most of the accommodation within the chapel, however, was for those who paid pew rents, which meant that many of the poorer members of the community still had to travel to Warblington. Services were conducted by a perpetual curate, although weddings and funerals were still the preserve of the parish church at Warblington. Despite its limitations, however, St Peter's Chapel represented an important step in the establishment of the town of Emsworth as a separate entity.

IV

1790–1840

'An improving, busy little place'

The long French war that began in 1793 led to an expansion of the Navy and brought unprecedented commercial opportunities to the mills and the shipyard in Emsworth. Edward Tollervey, a Portsmouth baker and businessman who had taken over Lumley Mill, secured a contract from the government to supply the Royal Navy at Portsmouth with pork and biscuits. With this as an incentive he turned the mill into a thriving integrated business. Corn meal that had been ground in the mill was baked into biscuits in a bakery he established on the site. The grist and spoiled biscuits were fed to pigs kept next to the mill, enabling him to supply both the pork and the biscuits from the one site. While the war lasted Tollervey's business was very profitable but there is evidence that once peace returned in 1815 he suffered a reverse in fortune.

Shipbuilding also benefited from the war. Although the Navy constructed its own warships in the Portsmouth dockyard, the Emsworth yard of Norris and King was well placed to secure orders to supply ships' boats and launches, boathooks, pike staves and capstan bars. The main work of the yard, however, remained the building of small fishing vessels and the larger coastal trading vessels. As in the 1780s, so in the 1790s the yard was exceptionally busy, completing 12 vessels during the decade. This level of activity continued into the new century, with a further eight vessels being launched in the years 1800-5. The years 1795 and 1802 were the busiest, with three vessels being launched in each. The average size of the vessels had also increased, no fewer than 11 of the ships built in the period 1790-1805 being brigs in excess of 90 tons and built for the growing coal trade. Thereafter the pace of activity in the shipyard began to slacken. Only 19 vessels were launched in the whole of the period 1805-40, of which just four were larger vessels, the majority being smaller ketches and sloops.

Emsworth's position as the largest port in Chichester Harbour was consolidated during this period. Farrant has shown that in 1836 171 of the 402 vessels that brought cargoes into the harbour were unloaded in the port of Emsworth. In that same year there were 392 outbound cargoes loaded in the harbour, of which 140 were loaded in Emsworth. Overall the port of Emsworth had captured some 40 per cent of the total volume of trade that was passing through Chichester Harbour by the late 1830s. By 1841 the number of vessels passing through the port had reached 274 per annum, an average of more than five each week.

The size of the Emsworth fishing industry can be gauged from the fact that in 1817 there were 30 fishing vessels based in the port. Most of these were the smaller 'jerkies' that were used for inshore fishing. The livelihoods of local fishermen, however, came under a growing threat from the activities of fishermen from the east coast ports sailing in larger fishing smacks. Writing in 1817, Walter Butler noted:

> The fishermen are deprived of their bread by fishing smacks from the eastern coast which, from their size and superiority of sailing, sweep the bottom of the sea and take away every oyster, and their success encourages them to defy the native fishermen, or run down his little boat, which gets entangled with the trawling tackle of the smacks. This unlawful fishing began about twenty years ago.

Because of overfishing the local oyster beds were exhausted by the early 19th century. One solution would have been greater regulation of the fishing grounds but the fishermen were opposed to this if it damaged their interests. In 1823 an Emsworth Fishery Bill, sponsored by the lord of the manor, was presented to Parliament. This Bill proposed to exclude any person from fishing in the harbour without a licence and to impose a duty on all fish caught. After a campaign of petitions the measure was defeated, prompting the *Hampshire Telegraph* of 10 May 1823 to describe 'the feelings of gratitude [felt] by the numerous poor Fishermen and their Families, whom this measure would have involved in so much difficulty and hapless poverty'. In the 1820s new oyster beds were discovered in the English Channel, off Shoreham, and increasingly Emsworth fishermen had to adapt themselves to offshore rather than inshore fishing.

By 1811 the population of Emsworth had grown to 1,358, and the 1841 census recorded a further increase to 1657. Whereas in the 1664-5 Hearth Tax return there were 52 households in Emsworth, this number had grown to 284 by 1811. As the town had become more prosperous employment opportunities had increased and the town had become able to support a larger population. A growing population meant increased house building. A visitor to modern Emsworth cannot fail to notice the number and the quality

21 *The Hut, King Street. This was the house built for John King in 1795.*

of the 18th- and early 19th-century buildings within the centre of the town. The schedule of listed buildings for the area contains no fewer than 68 buildings constructed in whole or in part during the late Georgian and Regency periods. A walker along Queen Street, King Street, Tower Lane, High Street, the Square, South Street and Nile Street will encounter many fine examples of the simple, classical lines and fine proportions of Georgian architecture. Of particular interest is the house called 'The Hut' in King Street which was built by John King in 1795 and was reputedly completed in one day. Most of these buildings were constructed of brick with tiled roofs and most were two storeys high, although there were some which stretched to three storeys. In the 1820s and 1830s a number of large, detached new 'villas' were built to the west of the town, along the Havant Road. All of these features

22   *A Georgian building in King Street.*

23   *An elegant doorway in a fine Georgian building in Queen Street.*

point to the existence in the town of several families who possessed substantial wealth. In the 1792 *Hampshire Directory* we learn that the town could support two lawyers, a clockmaker, one surgeon and two peruke (wig) makers, a sign that the town had a growing middle class. The 1831 *Pigot's Directory* shows that along the High Street and around the Square there were tailors, dressmakers, bootmakers, watchmakers, furniture and cabinet makers, a bookseller, two saddlers and a number of other small businesses that would have attracted a mainly middle-class clientele.

Among this section of Emsworth society the family name of Holloway deserves a special mention. The Holloways were an Emsworth family with a very long pedigree. The earliest known reference is on a 1495 rent roll which recorded that John Holloway rented a piece of land in Byrley field. The John Holloway who died in 1559 was a fisherman, as was the John Holloway who was fined one shilling by the manor court in 1687. In the Chichester Port Books a number of Holloways are recorded, from 1650 onwards, as being master mariners. By the

mid-18th century there were several branches of the family living in Emsworth, some of whom were mariners whilst others were involved in corn milling. A 1763 entry in the Manor Court Book records Benjamin, Thomas and Joseph Holloway as being in attendance. In the 1798 Land Tax assessment the family owned 25 properties and rented another; some of this property was around the junction of King Street and Queen Street. By the early 19th century Joseph Holloway was a successful merchant, John Holloway was a miller and Gawen Holloway had business and other interests. The Parish Overseer's Account Books for the 1820s show that he was a farmer of 229 acres (with a further 21 acres of rented land). He also ran a store in the High Street and was a brick maker and property developer. It was he who built several of the large villas along the Havant Road. Gawen Holloway was also prominent in parish business. He became a member of the new Select Vestry, made up of 'seventeen of the substantial householders … of this parish', which was established in 1819, and thus became involved in the administration of poor relief. By the end of the 19th century, however, the Holloways had disappeared from Emsworth society; the last surviving family member, Elizabeth, died in 1867.

Olivia Holloway was a leading member of the local Congregationalist (Independent) communion. In 1808 she was instrumental in the building of a new Congregational Chapel in Nile Street and she was also a regular preacher in the chapel, for which duties she always dressed entirely in white. Replacing an earlier place of Independent worship which had been situated in South Street, the new chapel was the only nonconformist chapel between Chichester and Havant. Its congregation therefore consisted not only of people from Emsworth itself but also from nearby villages such as Westbourne and Prinsted. Not everyone in Emsworth, however, welcomed this new addition; on one occasion the pulpit was stolen and dumped in the Hermitage millpond. Olivia herself left Emsworth for Stratford-upon-Avon in 1816.

James Cobby was another important figure in Emsworth society in the 1820s and 1830s. He appears in the 1831 *Directory* as the proprietor of a private day school for boys. He served the parish as constable for many years, at a time when the rural police had not yet been professionalised, and

24 *Slipper Millpond, looking towards Stakes Bridge, with Hermitage on the right. Dolphin Cut is on the left of the picture.*

he was also a churchwarden. He was the vice-president of the Emsworth Friendly Society in the 1840s and in 1857 he was recorded as being the town's post-master. The Cobbys appear to have lived in Emsworth for a number of generations. James himself was born in 1785, the son of James Cobby and Elizabeth Miller. The Cobby family name occurs in several places in West Sussex and the Emsworth branch of the family may have been descended from a James Cobbye who was born in Westbourne in 1592. As with the Holloways, however, the family name had all but disappeared from Emsworth by the end of the 19th century.

In an 1806 *Directory* Emsworth is described as 'a gay festive village with excellent subscription balls at the *Crown* and balls of a more humble nature at the *Black Dog*'. Balls were not the only diversion available to the more prosperous members of the local community at the beginning of the 19th century. Sea bathing had become fashionable towards the end of the 18th century and Robert Harfield, a local businessman who had established himself in Emsworth by 1792, built a bathing house beside the millpond on a corner of the common field known as 'Seafield'. This was available for rent. The status of sea bathing in Emsworth was enhanced in 1805 when Princess Caroline, who was staying nearby, was reported to have bathed in the town. When the bathing house was offered for sale some time later it was described as:

> a new erected BATHING HOUSE containing the necessary apartments for a small family, with two capacious baths, constantly supplied with fresh seawater, and dressing closets adjoining, with a furnace, pipes and apparatus for a hot bath. The above premises are standing by the waterside in Emsworth Harbour near the pleasant town of Emsworth.

Although Emsworth did not become a popular and fashionable sea bathing resort, the episode left its mark on the town. The road from the turnpike to the bathing house became known as Bathing House Road, since shortened to Bath Road.

Not every inhabitant of the town shared in this growing prosperity. Reference has already been made to the poverty of the fishermen and their families. Farm labourers, of whom there were still between 15 and 20 in the 1830s, were enduring a period of severe hardship in the years after the Napoleonic wars ended in 1815. Enclosure of the common fields had deprived them of their rights to keep animals on the common; the introduction of threshing machines was reducing the employment opportunities on farms. In addition, low prices for farm produce had driven labourers' wages down to a bare subsistence level. Some relief was provided by the parish in the form of a subsidy on wages – the so-called Speenhamland system. In 1823-4 the Warblington Parish Overseer's accounts show that the parish handed out £572 7s. 1d. in 'weekly pay'. By 1828-9 the amount paid out had fallen to £473 1s. 0d., but thereafter the cost of 'outdoor relief'

increased until it had reached £616 7s. 6d. in 1833-4. Local farmers and property owners who paid the poor rate were among those who felt that the burden of increasing rates could not be sustained and that reform of the Poor Law was necessary.

A parish 'poorhouse' had been established in Emsworth as early as 1738, probably housed in two cottages near the bottom of South Street. In 1776 a new and larger poorhouse was established in three cottages belonging to the lord of the manor in North Street. By 1814 there were 31 persons resident there, and in the 1820s the cost of 'victualling' for the 'poor in the house' was running at around £200 p.a. In 1834 a New Poor Law abolished the practice of giving the poor 'weekly pay' from the parish rates and also grouped parishes together into 'Unions' in which the relief of the poor was to be controlled by elected Boards of Guardians. Emsworth and Warblington became part of the Havant Union, which established a new workhouse in Havant. When the Havant workhouse opened the Emsworth poorhouse closed.

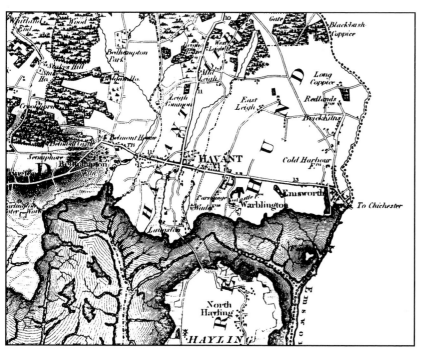

25 Greenwood's map, 1826. Brick kilns in the Redlands Farm area to the north of the town indicate one of the local industries. The seaside millpond is shown on the western side of Emsworth. The road pattern in the town itself has not been shown accurately. (Hampshire Record Office 139M89)

26 *Emsworth Square in the early 19th century. The parish pump, which was for many Emsworthians the main source of water, is in the middle of the picture. The man to the left of the pump with a handcart containing a barrel is probably a water-carrier. Note the white swan on an inn sign in the middle distance.*

Tensions in the farming community came to a head in 1830 when bands of farm labourers, gathering together under the banner of the mythical Captain Swing, began destroying threshing machines and setting fire to farm buildings and ricks across southern England. In November 1830 the disturbances spread to the Emsworth area. After attacking nine threshing machines in Emsworth and Havant the crowd assembled on the following day at Westbourne. There they were met with a show of force by the property owners and farmers of the district:

> The Havant magistrates heard this morning (19th November) that the mob that had attacked the machines in their district were meeting at Westbourne … Together with sixteen constables they proceeded to the village where they were joined by two Sussex magistrates accompanied by thirty of the Duke of Richmond's tenants, who were armed and mounted. They succeeded in apprehending nine men.

Military reinforcements were also brought in. Thirty men of the 47th Regiment were sent to Havant and a further 30 to Emsworth. The arrests, imprisonment and subsequent transportation of a number of the rioters, however, brought an end to the disturbances.

The disturbances were contained and the rioters punished, but the experience made a lasting impression on the governing classes. There was a noticeably more alarmist tone in the press reports in the 1830s. In December 1834, for example, a fire on the farm of Gawen Holloway, which destroyed two ricks, two barns, stables and a threshing machine, was reported by the *Hampshire Telegraph* as a clear case of politically motivated arson: 'There is no doubt of this being a most daring act of incendiarism, originating it is believed in the recent introduction of the New Poor Law Bill, in the operation of which this gentleman is engaged.'

The offer of a reward of 300 guineas, half of which was raised by public subscription and the other half from the Treasury, for information leading to the apprehension of the arsonist was a measure of the seriousness with which the incident was viewed. Even relatively minor outbreaks of trouble were reported as serious outrages by the *Hampshire Telegraph* in the more tense atmosphere of the 1830s. In May 1837 a night of drunken high spirits in Emsworth was reported thus:

> Emsworth and its vicinity has for some time past been the scene of occasional disturbances and depredations, committed by a set of drunken and profligate

characters, about midnight, after retiring from public houses and private resorts … Last Sunday [they] threw brickbats and stones at the bedroom window of the house of Mr Baker, Shoemaker of Emsworth, and broke seven panes of glass. [This] shows the absolute necessity for a local police in order to secure the apprehension of rogues who take advantage of darkness to destroy the property and disturb the peace of the neighbourhood.

Reported instances of crime were relatively rare in Emsworth, although some cases were referred to the Quarter Sessions in Winchester. Most of these cases involved petty thieving, suggesting a link with poverty. In 1807 John Phillips, aged 30, was charged with stealing 'one piece of cotton and several pairs of worsted stockings, well knowing the same to have been the property of John Bulbeck'. In 1808 Elizabeth Redman and her two daughters, aged 11 and 16, were charged with stealing shoes and other articles from the shop of John Phillips. Punishments for the convicted, however, were severe. In 1815 Jane Harris was sentenced to two months' imprisonment with hard labour for taking a calico sheet from the garden of Robert Maybee. Isaac Cobb received nine months' imprisonment with hard labour in

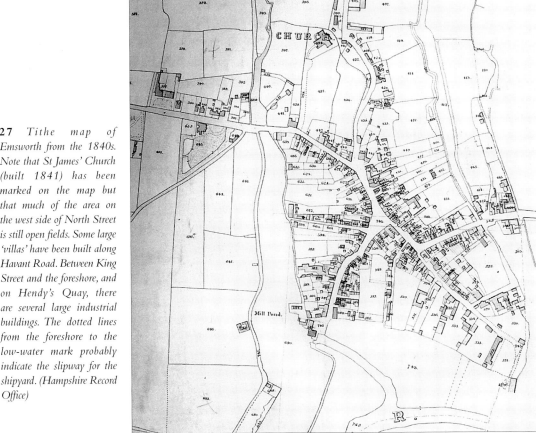

27 *Tithe map of Emsworth from the 1840s. Note that St James' Church (built 1841) has been marked on the map but that much of the area on the west side of North Street is still open fields. Some large 'villas' have been built along Havant Road. Between King Street and the foreshore, and on Hendy's Quay, there are several large industrial buildings. The dotted lines from the foreshore to the low-water mark probably indicate the slipway for the shipyard. (Hampshire Record Office)*

28 *These three cottages in North Street were used as the parish poorhouse between 1776 and the late 1830s.*

Education of the children of the poor was regarded as one means by which crime could be prevented. The first school for such children was established in 1812 by the Parish Overseers of the Poor and this was housed next to the poorhouse in North Street. By 1839 the school had moved to new premises in Bridgefoot Path and it had become a National School; in other words, it was being run under the auspices of the Church of England National Society for Promoting the Education of the Poor. It was written at the time that:

> This excellent institution bids fair to convey great benefits upon the neighbourhood and we may look forward with confidence to a general improvement of the morals and conduct of the lower classes of the community, whose instructions and improvement have hitherto been much neglected.

1835 for stealing two saws from William Stacey. The harshest punishment of all, however, was given in 1833 to the unfortunate Sarah Goodyer, a 20-year-old servant, for having stolen a cloak, other clothes, two brooches and one gold ring, to the value of £5; she was sentenced to seven years' transportation. The severity of this sentence probably reflects the more punitive approach to poverty and crime that had become evident in the 1830s. No full-time constable was appointed to police the town until the 1850s but the appeals of the *Hampshire Telegraph* did not go unheeded: in 1844 the number of part-time constables for the parish was increased to ten. All of these additional constables were drawn from the shopkeepers and small traders of the town.

In 1835 the school had 59 boys and 51 girls on its roll. The curriculum was limited to reading, writing and accounts together with religious instruction.

The 1831 *Pigot's Directory* described Emsworth as a 'respectable little market town', which was 'an improving, busy little place'. It noted that the dredging of oysters 'gives employment to many individuals of the industrious, humble class'. The town had also become noted for its part in a flourishing coastal trade, for ship and boat building, rope and sail making and for the range of other trades in which the people of the town were engaged. To outward appearances it was a prosperous and thriving community. For a significant proportion of its population, however, daily life still involved a hard struggle to make ends meet and avoid the ever-present threat of disease and destitution.

V

1840–1890

'So much life and bustle'

In March 1846 the *Hampshire Telegraph* reported on the state of trade through the port of Emsworth:

> The port of Emsworth has not exhibited so much life and bustle in the shipping line during the past twenty years as throughout the past week. Eleven fine brigs and schooners have been actively discharging their cargoes, the former of coals for various merchants, the latter of iron trams for the railway brought from Cardiff and Newport, at both of which ports many thousands of tons of iron are yet awaiting transmission to Emsworth.

> Cargoes of fine English fir, cut into sleepers, are being sent from this port to Southampton, there to be immersed in the preserving liquid, prior to be laid down on the Dorchester line.

Emsworth was about to enter the railway age. The building of the railway along the coast brought a short-term boost to the trade of the port, but would the long-term effects be quite so beneficial to the ship owners and mariners of the town?

In 1846 the Brighton and Chichester Railway Company had asked permission of the Parish Vestry of Warblington to build a railway line across

29 *Emsworth station. This signal box was built in the early 20th century to replace the original from 1847.*

North Street in Emsworth on the new route linking Brighton with Portsmouth. Permission was granted on condition that a new station be built by the side of North Street 'with accommodation and appearance not less than that of the station at Fareham', and that all passenger trains, with the exception of expresses, were to stop there. The line was opened on 15 March 1847. The Brighton and Chichester Railway Company was quickly absorbed into the larger network of the London, Brighton and South Coast Railway Company. Small towns such as Emsworth were thus connected to a growing national railway network. *Bradshaw's Railway Guide* of 1849 shows that there were five trains a day between Brighton and Portsmouth. Ordnance Survey maps from later in the century show that Emsworth station had a goods siding and cattle pens. For both passenger travel and for freight transport, therefore, the railway offered new opportunities and new challenges for the town.

The LB&SCR had an arrangement with the London and North Western Railway Company to transport coal from Staffordshire onto its network in southern England. Staffordshire coal, delivered by railway truck to the sidings at Emsworth station, thus began to compete with the Durham coal brought by sea. By the end of the century the local coal merchant, W. Foster and Co., was buying wagonloads of coal from South Yorkshire to be delivered to Emsworth station. The opening of the railway, however, did not lead to the immediate demise of the seaborne trade in coal. In the 1840s, according to Daly's estimate, the port of Emsworth handled about 10,000 tons of coal annually. In the second half of the century the demand for coal in Emsworth, as elsewhere, was increasing. As well as the growing demand for coal for domestic use there was also demand from the new gasworks, opened in 1854, from the brickworks, and from the owners of steam traction engines and steam-driven saw mills, which made their appearance in the town towards the end of the century. This increased demand can be seen in the growth in the number of coal merchants in the town. Whereas in *Pigot's Directory* of 1831 there are two coal merchants listed, the 1857 *Craven's Directory* lists no fewer than five.

Seaborne trade in coal, therefore, survived the coming of the railway and continued into the 20th century. Indeed, so confident were the local ship owners and coal merchants that this trade would continue that they were still investing in new vessels in the 1850s and 1860s. The *Indian*

30 *Emsworth station. This picture, taken in the Edwardian period, shows the Station Master's house next to the main entrance to the station.*

LONDON to BRIGHTON, LEWES, HASTINGS, & PORTSMOUTH.—London, Brighton, and South Coast.
Sec., T. J. Buckton, Tooley-st.   G. Hawkins, Goods Manager.   J. Pountain, Sup. Passenger Traffic.

(Down Trains timetable — five trains each day, with Sundays and Fares columns, for stations: London Bridge, New Cross, Forest Hill, Croydon, Stoat's Nest, Reigate, Horley, Three Bridges Jun, Crawley, Fay Gate, Horsham arr., Hayward's Heath, Burgess Hill, Hassock's Gate, BRIGHTON arr., Hayward's Heath dep., Lewes, Hastings arrival, Brighton departure, Southwick, Shoreham, Worthing, Angmering, Littlehampton, Arundel, Bognor, Drayton, Chichester, Emsworth, Havant arrival, Portsmouth.)

† First, Second, and Third Class from Brighton.

Day Tickets are issued at London, New Cross, and Croydon, on Saturdays and Sundays, by all the trains to Brighton, and Stations beyond, entitling the holders to return by any Train of the same class, either on Sunday or Monday.

PORTSMOUTH, HASTINGS, LEWES, BRIGHTON, &c. to LONDON.—London, Brighton, and S. Coast.
Res. Eng., R. J. Hood.   G. Smith, Carriage Supt.   Loco. Sup., J. C. Craven.

(Up Trains timetable — with Sundays and Fares columns, for stations: Portsmouth, Havant, Emsworth, Chichester, Drayton, Bognor, Arundel, Littlehampton, Angmering, Worthing, Shoreham, Southwick, Hove, Hastings dep., Lewes, Hayward's Heath, Brighton arrival, Ditto departure, Hassock's Gate, Burgess Hill, Hayward's Heath, Balcombe, Horsham dep., Fay Gate, Crawley, Three Bridges, Horley, Reigate, Stoat's Nest, Croydon, Forest Hill, New Cross, London Bridge arr.)

Fare between London & Brighton by Parliamentary trains 4s. 2d.

* First Class only from Brighton.   † First and second class only from Brighton.   ‡ Mail, 1 and 2 class from Brighton.
The stations at which Carriages & Horses can be loaded or unloaded are marked thus*.—No carriages or horses will be taken by 1¼ hour trains, at 5 aft. down, and 8¾ morn. up.

31 *A page from* Bradshaw's Railway Guide, *1849. The timetable shows five trains each day in either direction. A journey to London via Brighton took at least four hours (and even longer on some services).*

Queen was a 72-ton schooner built in Emsworth in 1859 for W. Foster. Between 1859 and 1871 Foster and his business partner, Elijah Packer, took delivery of another nine ships that were built for the coal trade, including the *Jane E. Foster* (1861), the *Elijah Packer* (1863), the *Mayflower* (1865) and the *Thorney Island* (1871). In the early 1860s the King family also acquired three new vessels for their coal business. Coal merchants and ship

owners at other ports along the coast were also investing in new ships at this time. Clarke and Hellyer of Havant, for example, were buying ships from shipyards in Sunderland, as were ship owners in Portsmouth and Fareham.

None of this suggests an industry in decline. In fact, in the 1860s and 1870s the seaborne coal trade seems to have been at its height. The Crew Lists and Half-Yearly Agreements, which were first

32   *Emsworth from the harbour. This 1850s print shows a busy harbour scene with a schooner lying at anchor and several fishing boats at work.*

33   *The* Emma Louise. *Built in Emsworth in the 1870s, this fine vessel was used for the coal trade.*

34 *The* Indian Queen. *A 72-ton schooner built in Emsworth in 1859 for William Foster, this vessel was employed for many years in the coal trade with the north-eastern ports.* Indian Queen *was lost with all hands off the Farne Islands in 1893.*

introduced in 1863, show the extent of the trading voyages made by Emsworth-owned vessels at this time. The north-east ports were still the most common sources of supply for coal. Sunderland, Hartlepool, Seaham, Middlesbrough, South Shields

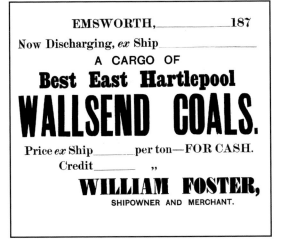

35 *Wallsend Coal. This handbill was printed for William Foster, one of Emsworth's main coal merchants, to advertise the sale of coal brought into Emsworth from the north east.*

and Newcastle were regularly visited by both Foster's and King's vessels. Occasional visits were made to Scottish ports and an increasing number of cargoes were shipped from the South Wales coal ports of Cardiff, Neath, Llanelli, Newport and Swansea. On outward voyages the ships often carried cargoes of timber, such as planks, wedges or pit props. Not all of the return voyages were to Emsworth. Some of Foster's vessels were at times fully engaged in transporting cargoes of coal to Portsmouth. There were also many visits to the small ports around Chichester Harbour, the Isle of Wight, Fareham and ports along the Solent. Across the Channel the French ports, Le Havre, Caen and St Malo, and the Channel Island ports were all supplied with coal transported on Foster and Packer's and King's vessels. There were also voyages to more distant ports: the *Indian Queen* was trading in the Mediterranean in 1863; the *Mayflower* made voyages to the Baltic in 1869 and 1870; the *Thorney Island* visited the White Sea port of Archangel in 1873. When these vessels were not engaged in the coal trade there were other bulk cargoes to be shifted. Welsh slate from Porthmadoc, Cornish stone from Penrhyn and

36 *The goods siding at Emsworth station. This late 19th-century photograph shows a single goods siding and a goods shed.*

Dorset clay from Poole were all carried on these Emsworth vessels at one time or another.

The Emsworth quays were kept very busy in the 1860s and 1870s. In 1866, for example, eight vessels owned by local coal merchants brought a total of 32 shipments of coal to Emsworth. In 1876 seven vessels brought 23 shipments, but a decade later a mere three vessels brought 17 shipments. Thereafter the records show that the trade in coal through the port of Emsworth continued to decline, although the port was still receiving regular shipments of coal in the years leading up to the outbreak of war in 1914. This trend is reflected in the actions of local coal merchants and ship owners. Having bought several new

vessels in the years 1859-71, Foster and Packer began to dispose of much of their fleet in the late 1870s. Between 1879 and 1881 Foster and Packer sold six of their vessels to owners in Portsmouth and elsewhere. Thereafter these vessels did not trade through Emsworth.

Competition from the railway was only one of the problems facing the trade. The shallow waters of Chichester Harbour, particularly over the bar at the entrance, restricted the size of vessels that could trade in and out of Emsworth. The *Indian Queen* was a topsail schooner of 72 tons whilst the *Victoria L. Foster* was 109 tons. At 184 tons the *Thorney Island* was the largest coal vessel to call at Emsworth, although this vessel spent most

37 *A coal wagon belonging to Ewens Brothers of Emsworth. It was common in the early 20th century for coal merchants to own or lease their own railway wagons. Foster and Co. had their own fleet of coal wagons.*

38 *Gosden Green windmill. Gosden Green is situated about one mile to the east of Emsworth.*

of its working life trading out of Portsmouth. As sailing vessels they were subject to the vagaries of wind direction and other hazards. In 1874, for example, the *Indian Queen* was stranded for a time off Whitby; in 1893 this same vessel was lost with all hands off the Farne Islands. Between 1866 and 1897 no fewer than eight Emsworth-owned ships involved in the coal trade were lost at sea. Yet despite the risks, such vessels could still be operated at a profit in the favourable trading conditions of the late 19th century.

Corn milling and the 'export' of flour and malt through the port had also been mainstays of the local economy in the 18th and early 19th centuries. Here again trading conditions were changing. The end of the French wars had drastically reduced orders for naval victualling from Portsmouth, and the opening of the Navy's own mill and bakery at Gosport in 1838 further reduced demand for flour from local mills. On the other hand, the rapidly growing population and the associated expansion of the large towns created an ever-increasing demand for food. Local mills continued to operate throughout these changing trading conditions. Indeed, in 1865 a fifth mill was added when the new Slipper Tide Mill was opened to the south of the existing Slipper Tide Mill. It was built by Andrew Bone Hatch, who

was described in the 1857 *Craven's Directory* as a miller at the Quay Mill, a maltster, coal merchant and farmer. As well as owning the Quay Mill at this time he also owned the Gosden Green windmill. Clearly he was a businessman of some standing in the local community. The windmill was abandoned in the 1860s, possibly because such mills were more expensive to maintain than water mills, and Hatch invested in the new Slipper Tide Mill, just before the industry was exposed to the full blast of competition from America. This alone would almost certainly have rendered the new mill a commercial failure, but its problems were compounded by serious technical weaknesses. The new mill could not develop its full power because the flow of water from the existing Slipper Mill was already reduced. Later a steam engine was installed in an attempt to provide additional power but the mill was never fully operational. The millpond passed into the hands of J.D. Foster, who used it for seasoning timber.

Attempts were made to modernise the other mills in order to face the growing competition. By 1895 the Town Mill was owned by Chatfield and Co., and *Kelly's Directory* of that year tells us that this mill was operated by both water and steam. The mill had been completely destroyed by

39 *Slipper Mill. This late 19th-century view shows the grain store of the mill with the tidal mill building at right angles to it. A barge is tied up alongside. The chimney on the right belonged to the ill-fated mill built by Andrew Bone Hatch in 1865. (EMHT/ Mountfield)*

fire in 1894, and when it was rebuilt a horizontal water turbine was installed to replace the old water wheel. This was a much more efficient means of powering the mill. By the end of the century the Quay Mill had been equipped with a steam engine to provide auxiliary power when the millpond was too low to drive the wheel. At Lumley Mill, too, a steam engine was installed; the Slipper Mill, on the other hand, continued to be reliant on the tidal race from the millpond. All of these mills operated until 1914. Lumley Mill, however, was completely destroyed by fire in 1915 and was never rebuilt.

The numbers directly employed in corn milling were relatively small. The 1841 census records only six persons in Emsworth who gave their occupation as milling. In 1881 there were nine men employed in Emsworth mills and a further three in the Hermitage. In addition to those directly employed there were the carters who travelled between the local mills and transported the grain from the farms and corn merchants.

Other local businesses also managed to survive. A study of the trade directories reveals a rich and varied pattern of businesses that supplied most of the needs of the town's population. In 1857 there were seven bootmakers, four dressmakers, four tailors, three cabinet makers and one watchmaker. There were also sailmakers, ropemakers, brewers and maltsters, a gunsmith and a cycle manufacturer trading in the town. Although the peruke makers of the late 18th century did not survive the changes in fashion, other traditional craftsmen such as cordwainers (leather workers) were still well represented in the town during the first half of the 19th century. Nine men gave their occupation as cordwainer in the 1841 census, but there were only four in 1861 and just one in 1881. In 1841 there were two pipemakers and one nail maker recorded in the census. Taplin's pipe-making business continued to appear in the trade directories until 1857. These directories also mention, at various times, a chairmaker, a wheelwright, a cooper and a hoop maker. As the century wore on the pattern of local manufacturing changed. Partly this was the result of changes in technology which rendered many old crafts such as cordwaining redundant, but it was also due to the growing influx of

40 *The Town Mill. This Victorian photograph shows the loading of carts with sacks of milled flour.*

cheaper, mass-produced goods made elsewhere. The decline in local bootmaking and tailoring, for example, illustrates this trend. Sailmaking, ropemaking and other trades associated with the local shipbuilding industry, on the other hand, remained important local industries throughout the 19th century and a coachbuilder appears in *Kelly's Directory* for 1875.

The fishing industry grew to an unprecedented size and importance during the second half of the 19th century. The *Craven Directory* of 1857 emphasised the importance of the oyster trade to the town:

> The oyster trade bears an important feature in the prosperity of the town. Emsworth has for a long period been noted for its oysters and beds having been formed in the deeps … and great quantities are forwarded to London, besides supplying the towns in the neighbourhood.

By the early 1840s, however, the Emsworth oyster fishermen faced mounting problems. With growing competition from east coast fishermen and from the French and the Dutch, the middle decades of the 19th century were a difficult time for local fishermen. One response to the growing competition was to establish private oyster beds within Chichester and Langstone Harbours. This process was expensive and involved ancient property rights so could not be undertaken by ordinary fishermen. In the 1840s the lords of the manors of Hayling and Farlington granted portions of the mud flats in the harbours for the establishment of private oyster beds in the Crastick Channel, in Langstone Harbour and at Mill Rythe off the coast of North Hayling, all areas where Emsworth fishermen had traditionally dredged for oysters. In a letter to the *Hampshire Telegraph*, entitled 'The Oyster Monopoly', one local fisherman complained thus:

> The oyster monopolists have destroyed the hitherto unrivalled oyster beds of Emsworth … Here the channels have been swept clean, both of market ware and of brood oysters, which have been carried to and laid down in the beds …

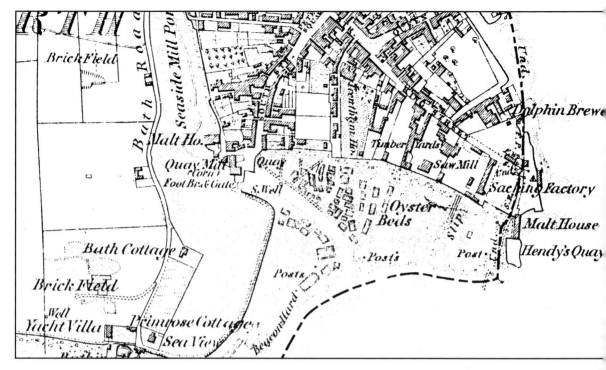

41   *O.S. map, 1870. On this section of the map the development of King Street as an industrial area can be clearly seen. Timber yards, a saw mill, a sacking factory, a brewery and a malt house were all situated along this street. On the foreshore, of which a great deal is occupied by the oyster beds, the 'slip' indicates the location of the shipyard. To the west of the Seaside millpond there are two brick fields, signs of another local industry. (Hampshire Record Office)*

and they are now unfairly considered a private property.

Emsworth fishermen refused to recognise the private property rights of the owners of the oyster beds and continued to dredge at Mill Rythe. According to Longcroft, the Emsworth fishermen 'attacked in a body the various oyster-layings, beginning with that belonging to the Russells in Crastick Lake'. Twenty-two of them were arrested and imprisoned in Winchester Jail. At their subsequent trial eight were convicted of illegally dredging for oysters.

This dispute between the fishermen, who were determined to exercise and protect what they considered to be their ancient rights to dredge in the harbour, and the private interests, who were seeking to establish exclusive rights over sections of the sea bed, rumbled on for more

than 30 years. Regulation of oyster fishing began in 1843, when a Convention between the British and French governments banned the dredging of oysters between 1 May and 30 September of each year. This was designed to prevent overfishing of the oyster beds, but a report in the *Hampshire Telegraph* on the opening of the 1845 oyster fishing season made clear that the east coast fishermen still posed a threat to local fishermen:

On 1st September the Emsworth Fishery Season opened, when the usual depredations were perpetrated by about eighty sail of smacks, chiefly from Colchester, Rochester, etc., some of them averaging fifty tons and carrying crews of six men and a boy. In four days they cleared every channel and left but little behind to repay the small boats for their

42   *The Emsworth foreshore in the late 19th century. In the foreground the oyster beds can clearly be seen. The men in the picture are collecting oysters for sale under the watchful eye of their employer, possibly J.D. Foster. In the background are the steam saw mill belonging to Sparks and, to the right, a large shed that was part of the shipyard.*

hard and constant labour throughout the ensuing winter.

The newspaper's call for greater legislative protection for the local fisheries, however, went unheeded. Local fishermen faced a further encroachment on their ancient rights in 1850 when an extensive area of the mud flats in Langstone, Emsworth and Chichester Harbours were enclosed. This scheme, which was sponsored by the lordships of local manors, was promoted on the grounds that it would help control the flow of tidal waters and lead to the deepening of the navigation channels. Local fishermen, however, complained that they would be excluded from yet

more areas of the harbour and that the natural oyster beds would become buried under layers of mud, and they put up a vigorous, though unsuccessful, resistance to the enclosure.

The disputes over the enclosure of areas of the harbour echoed the controversies that had surrounded the enclosure of common land in the 18th and early 19th centuries. On the one hand there were those who exercised customary rights to unrestricted access to the harbour. On the other side were the lords of the manors, who were asserting their property rights based on ancient charters. There was no dispute over the ownership of the foreshore – this had long been accepted as being the property of the lords of the manors. The new element in the 19th century was the assertion by these lords that their ownership extended beyond the low-water mark to mid-channel in the harbour. As with the common rights of farm labourers so it was with the fishermen: the inability of the small independent fishermen to prove their legal title to their fishing rights and the greater financial resources of the lords of the manors ensured that the latter held sway.

Conflict again broke out in the 1870s. The formation of the Emsworth Oyster Company, and the grant to it by Parliament of exclusive rights over 45 acres of the harbour, caused controversy within the town. The fishermen complained that, although 45 acres was only a small part of their total fishing grounds, the area selected was the most productive part of the harbour for oyster fishing. In May 1870 the secretary of the Emsworth Oyster Company, Thomas Jarman, claimed he was assaulted by one of the local fishermen and that others had set a dog on him because 'he was robbing the local fishermen'. Giving evidence at the subsequent trial the local police constable said that the town had been 'in a very excited state' over the issue. The fisherman in this case was found guilty of assault and the Emsworth Oyster Merchants' Company was successful in its petition to Parliament for the oyster grounds. In the following year another local fisherman, Richard Savage, was brought to trial and convicted of unlawfully dredging for shrimp on an oyster fishery at North Hayling, the property of the South of England Oyster Company. With property interests and the law ranged against them, Emsworth fishermen decided that the best defence of their interests was through co-operation and regulation. They formed themselves into the Emsworth Dredgermen's Co-operative Society (EDCS) and applied to the Board of Trade for the Emsworth Fishery Order of 1871 which gave them 'the right of several fishery over a large portion of the Emsworth Channel'. The granting of this order gave the small fishermen

some legal protection, although disputes between the EDCS and the Emsworth Oyster Merchants' Company over fishing rights continued into the 1890s, when the latter was finally wound up. The EDCS was still in existence in 1914, at which time it had 73 members. Fishermen could become members between the ages of 18 and 20 on payment of a £1 entrance fee, although in practice membership was limited to the traditional fishing families.

Sporadic resistance by individual fishermen to the dividing up of the sea bed continued through the 1870s. In 1872 Stephen and John Goldring were charged with assault on the Superintendent of the South of England Oyster Company, following a dispute over the ownership of some oyster ponds. In 1877 the South of England Oyster Company again summoned two local fishermen, Richard Prior and John Boutell, for unlawfully dredging over their oyster beds. After this, however, no further such cases were reported in the local press. Greater regulation and the creation of private oyster beds seem to have become accepted as the way forward for the oyster industry.

When J.D. Foster became an oyster merchant in the 1870s he bought oyster ponds on the Emsworth foreshore and at Mill Rythe from W. Cribb. He also purchased smaller oyster beds from individual fishermen. Foster was one of the key figures in the growth of the Emsworth oyster trade in the last decades of the 19th century. The son of William Foster, a prominent local coal merchant and ship owner, James Duncan Foster started his own oyster and scallop business in the late 1870s whilst only 21 years old. In 1879 he purchased three small fishing vessels from James Cribb: the *Jane* (23 tons), the *Jack Tar* (15 tons) and the *Lady of the Lake* (26 tons). After both the *Jane* and the *Jack Tar* were wrecked in successive years, 1880 and 1881, he decided to go into the shipbuilding business on his own account. In the mid-1880s, he started his own yard on Hendy's Quay. He purchased timber from

43 *An artists's impression of an Emsworth fishing boat of the 19th century. This painting appears on the wall of a house in Queen Street.*

local estates and transported it to Emsworth for seasoning in seawater in the Dolphin Lake. He also established his own saw mill, driven by a steam engine. With these facilities in place he embarked, in the late 1880s, on a programme of building his own larger fishing ketches. The first of these was the *Evolution*, a 55-ton ketch launched in 1888. This was followed in 1889 by the *Thistle* and, in 1890, by *Sybil* and *Ostrea*. Foster was beginning to equip himself with a fleet of modern sailing fishing vessels designed for dredging for oysters in the English Channel and further afield.

J.D. Foster had established his own shipbuilding yard to build a fleet of fishing vessels. His father had previously taken over the King Street yard of David Palmer Walker, who had owned the yard from 1844 to 1855, during which time he built at least two vessels of some considerable size. The first of these was a 407-ton barque, the

Frances Walker, built in the 1840s. Following this a much larger vessel, the 616-ton *Adelaide,* was laid down in the 1850s, but the vessel was not launched until 1857, after Walker's death. The *Hampshire Telegraph* of 17 January 1857 reported the launch thus:

> [Launched] from the premises of the late Mr David Palmer Walker, in the presence of a large concourse of spectators, a fine ship, the largest known to be built at this port, of 616 tons old measurement, the property of Messrs. Kay of Landport.

William Foster was a coal merchant and ship owner, not a shipbuilder, and the responsibility for the construction of vessels in his yard had been, until the 1870s, in the hands of a shipwright, Joseph Edgar. In the 1875 edition of *Kelly's Directory* the name of George Apps appears as the shipwright. By the 1880s the yard was being referred to as belonging to Apps. A member of the Apps family from Bosham, George came with established credentials as a shipwright and his arrival coincided with a change in the shipbuilding business in Emsworth. After the *Adelaide* was launched in 1857, the yard completed orders for five large brigs and two schooners in the next 18 years. Thereafter the yard completed seven vessels between 1875 and 1880, but they were all of a smaller size, displacing 20 to 30 tons in the main. The days of constructing large brigs were all but over.

Emsworth was, first and foremost, a seafaring town. Census returns show that fishing was the largest single source of male employment in the town for the whole of the period 1840-90. No fewer than 70 men gave their occupation as fisherman in the 1881 census. A further 38 were listed as mariners. Across the river in Hermitage there were a further four fishermen and 14 mariners in 1881. When the six shipwrights and the 10 men and seven boys employed in Albert Tatchell's sail and ropemaking business are also included, it is clear that a high proportion of families' livelihoods depended on the fishing industry and seaborne trade. Provisioning of the ships for sea brought valuable business for local shops. Special half-gallon loaves were supplied for the ships' crews by the bakers of the town, particularly Davis of Queen Street. Salt beef was supplied by two main butchers, Mant and Clayton. Coal merchants were still largely dependent on supplies brought in by sea. Many local business people also had a direct financial interest in the ships that traded through Emsworth. Although William Foster was the leading ship owner in the town for much of the period 1840-90, he was in partnership with Elijah Packer, described as a 'gentleman'. The ownership of some of their vessels was shared with others. The *Mayflower,* for example, was half-owned by Foster and Packer, and a Mr Caldwell of Havant owned a further quarter share. William Foster owned 40/64 of the *Indian Queen;* 16/64 were owned by William Tier, an Emsworth grocer; the remaining 8/64 were held by Mr Orton of Havant. The grocer John Blackmore and the coal merchant Henry Hall both owned shares in the *Dispatch* and in the *Emsworth.* Sometimes the ships' masters owned shares in the vessels they commanded, as with William Prewett of the *Dispatch.* Local innkeepers were also involved. Shared ownership was a way of spreading the risk involved in coastal trade as well as sharing out the profits. The effect was to reinforce the links that existed within the local business community and to ensure that dependence on the sea reached into every layer of Emsworth society.

VI

1840–1890

'A small and healthy town'?

In 1841 Emsworth took a further step towards establishing a separate identity from Warblington when it became a separate district within the parish and a new church, St James's, was built. The ecclesiastical independence of Emsworth was finally confirmed in 1866 when the parish of St James became entirely separate from that of Warblington. As the century wore on, however, the lack of any real control for local people over their civil affairs became a growing frustration.

The population of Emsworth continued to grow through the Victorian period but not at a steady rate, as the table shows:

44 *St James's Church. A print from the 1840s showing the church as it was originally built.*

Census Year	1841	1861	1881
Emsworth (population)	1,657	1,868	1,780
Emsworth and Warblington	2,270	2,196	2,374

(The Census Reports for 1841 and 1861 give population figures for Emsworth of 1,165 and 1,655 respectively. The figures used in this table are taken from the census enumerators' books which give a street-by-street, household-by-household survey of the population. An area which included Nile Street, Mill Pond, Havant Road, part of North Street and West Street is included in the Warblington figures in the final report but is correctly given as Emsworth in the enumerators'

45 *St James's Church. The modern appearance of the building.*

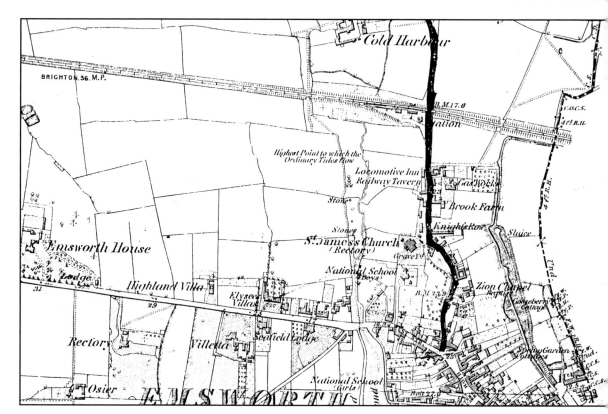

46   *The 1870 O.S. map. This section of the map shows the railway line and station, the gasworks in North Street, and the National (Church) school for boys next to the church. A Zion (Baptist) chapel has been built in North Street. (Hampshire County Record Office)*

books.) Part of this population growth was due to migration into the town, but most of the people who settled in Emsworth during this period had not moved very far. In 1881 some 53 per cent of the town's population had been born in Emsworth itself, with another 30 per cent coming from within a 10-mile radius. The census returns for this period show very clearly that the families who lived in High Street and the Square, and those in South Street, Orange Row, Seaside, Nile Street and Tower Street, were mainly families who had lived in Emsworth for generations. South Street, Seaside and Nile Street were inhabited overwhelmingly by fishermen, mariners and their families. House after house was occupied by various branches of the Parham, Farndell, Boutell, Dridge, Randell, Prior, Kennett, Dawkins, Wells, Duke and Jones families. All Emsworth-

born members of these families tended to marry within their own community, the males following the profession of their fathers and grandfathers. This created a very close-knit community. Even within this section of the community, however, the pressure to find employment, or marriage, led some to move elsewhere. The 1881 census records seven members of the Jones family, five Farndells, four Randells, four Kennetts and five Dawkins as living elsewhere. The majority of those who moved away from Emsworth settled in the local area. Portsmouth was a powerful economic magnet, especially for men engaged in maritime occupations. Although further away, London was also an area to which a significant number of Emsworth people, particularly craftsmen, were drawn, and perhaps the attraction of moving to London had increased after the opening of the railway line through Emsworth in 1847. Very few Emsworth people seem to have moved further afield although there were some interesting examples of long-distance migration. Edward Tier, for example, had settled in Pontefract, Yorkshire, and was described as a bookseller, stationer and dealer in 'Berlin wool'. William Wells was plying his trade as a mariner and living in Mylor, Cornwall, as was John Dawkins, who was earning his living as a scripture reader. William Newell was working as a Baptist minister near Bristol, Henry Randell was a dock labourer in Liverpool and Martha Taylor was a 'felt hat trimmer' in Bury, Lancashire. Arthur Hatch, a relative of Andrew Bone Hatch, was a brewer in Paignton, Devon.

King Street was the main industrial area of the town with its shipyards, saw mills and rope and sailmaking factory. It was also the street where many of the important business leaders of the town had taken up residence. Here, in 1881, were the houses of two branches of the King family, the Fosters and the Tatchells. Alongside them were shipwrights, a blacksmith, a butcher, a bootmaker and a tailor. Some of the fine Georgian houses in Queen Street were occupied by families living on 'independent means', but also in the street were a doctor, a watchmaker, two bootmakers, two shipwrights and an agricultural labourer. High Street and St Peter's Square made up the main commercial centre of the town, with numerous inns, grocers, bakers, butchers, drapers, tailors, and a variety of other small businesses. North Street had a similar mixture of small businesses, such as a coach builder, and residential properties that were home to various artisans, particularly bricklayers, carpenters, a gasmaker, a blacksmith and a chimney sweep. In these areas Emsworth-born residents still predominated, but, between 1861 and 1901, there was a noticeable increase in the number of heads of household who had been born elsewhere.

The Tatchell family were not originally from Emsworth, but by the mid-19th century the family business was one of the town's leading employers. James Tatchell had been born in 1791 in Donhead St Mary, Wilts., the son of a saddler and harness maker. He had moved to Emsworth in 1820 where he married Catherine Saxby, a descendant of John King, and set up his rope and sailmaking business. He became active in parish affairs, being a member of the Select Vestry and, in 1843, the Surveyor of the Highways. He also played a leading role in the town's business affairs and was one of the founders of the Emsworth Gas Company in the 1850s. After his death in 1876 his son, Albert, took over the business and ran it as a successful enterprise, supplying local ship owners, farmers, millers, and even churches with items as diverse as sails, sacking, binding twine and bell ropes. Albert Tatchell was elected to be a Poor Law Guardian in the Havant Union and for many

47 *Albert Tatchell (1840-1915). Albert took over the family rope and sailmaking business in King Street from his father James Tatchell. He became prominent in local political affairs as a member (and later Chairman) of the Havant Union Board of Guardians and was also a member of the Warblington Urban District Council.*

years served as the chairman of that body. He was also one of the first elected members of the Warblington Urban District Council from 1895. When he retired from business in 1905 he sold the company to Carter and Lewis, who continued to operate from the King Street premises for many years.

Since the late 18th century there had been a noticeable trend for relatively wealthy families to settle in and around the town. The 1792 *Directory* lists 23 persons described as 'gentry'. By 1871 the number listed had increased to 35, and in 1903 there were 131 persons described as 'private residents'. Included in this group were retired naval and army officers, of whom there were six in 1831 and nine in 1903. 'Gentry' households were scattered throughout the town, with a number in Queen Street, others in King Street, Tower Street, High Street and West Street. The wealthier families, however, favoured the more rural areas on the northern and western sides of

the town. Large detached 'villas' along the Havant Road, such as Highland Villa, Western Villa and Emsworth House, and in the Coldharbour area, such as North Villa and Lawn Villa, were built during the mid-19th century. These households invariably employed a number of domestic servants. At Holly Bank House, for example, a retired colonial administrator employed no fewer than five servants; at Emsworth House, Captain Boyd of the 1st Middlesex Militia had nine; the Rectory had six; a Deputy Judge Advocate of the Fleet, living at Highland Villa, employed three.

The employment of living-in servants was not confined to the 'gentry' families but extended to the middle classes as well. Albert Tatchell's household in King Street employed three domestic servants, William King had two and William Foster one. Many of the shopkeepers and small traders in the town could also afford to keep at least one servant, as could schoolmasters, doctors and lawyers. In 1861 there were 45 households in

48 *Victorian 'villas' along New Brighton Road.*

49 *A class photograph from Emsworth church school, late 19th century. By the time this photograph was taken the girls' and boys' schools had merged. (EMHT/Rashleigh)*

the town which had at least one servant. In the 1881 census no fewer than 138 women and girls were employed as domestic servants, by far the largest single source of employment for single women. Other adult and mainly married women contributed to the family income by working from their own homes as laundresses or washerwomen. There was also a growing number of men who were employed as gardeners at the larger houses around the area, and a smaller number who were employed as grooms.

As the population of Emsworth grew more rapidly than that of Warblington the characters of the two communities increasingly diverged. This was reflected in the growing feeling among the people of the town that more of their needs could best be catered for within their own community. A major step in this direction was taken in 1841 when the new church, St James's, was built on the site of an old brickfield owned by Gawen Holloway in the north-western part of the town. One third of the £1,900 cost of the new church was raised by public subscription and among the subscribers were such prominent local families as the Parhams, the Tiers and the Whichers. Unlike St Peter's Chapel the new church was allowed to offer the full range of religious services, including marriages, baptisms

and burials. It was also different from the earlier 'Proprietary' chapel in that the majority of its 566 seats were free, and therefore the new place of worship was more accessible to the poor of the parish. Both chapel and church, however, shared the same minister, the Reverend H.W. Sheppard. For a few years, therefore, Emsworth was in the unusual position for such a small community of having two separate places of worship for the Anglican community, with a total of 1,066 places between them. This situation was untenable in the long term, however, and in 1852 St Peter's Chapel closed. This was followed by the expansion of pew sittings at St James's Church so that by 1858 it could seat 744 persons.

The 1840s also saw growing efforts by the nonconformists to establish a strong presence in the town. The Congregationalists, or Independents, had established their own place of worship in Nile Street in 1808, replacing an earlier chapel that had been in Saffron Hill. The Baptists were also well established in the town, especially among artisans, but they had no chapel of their own until 1848, when the Zion Chapel was opened in North Street. Primitive Methodists were also making an attempt to establish themselves in Emsworth in the 1840s, although initially with little success. Primitive Methodist preachers from their mission

50   *The Emsworth Baptist Church, in North Street, as it appears today.*

church in Petersfield were conducting services in Emsworth by 1844 but the mission was abandoned in 1845 due to lack of support. It was not until 1876 that the Chichester Mission succeeded in establishing a Methodist Society in Emsworth and early results were so promising that the Methodist Church in the Square was opened in 1877. In the intervening years the nearest place of worship for Emsworth Methodists was in Havant. Similarly, any Catholics living in Emsworth had to travel to Brockhampton for their spiritual needs until 1875, when the Catholic church was opened in West Street. There was also a small group of Calvinistical Protestants who had a meeting room in the Square in the 1850s.

The 1851 Religious Census enables us to gain an insight into the state of churchgoing in Emsworth at that time. The Anglican churches in the town attracted by far the majority of churchgoers, with 181 attending St Peter's

Chapel and 365 St James's Church for morning service. The Baptist Chapel recorded 202 and the Congegationalist Chapel in Nile Street had 84. Using a formula employed by the census takers we can conclude that around 62 per cent of the population of Emsworth attended church or chapel at least once on census day. Even by the standards of the time this was a high figure. Victorian society was shocked to learn that nationally the proportion of the population who attended church was as low as 41 per cent. The Anglican share of church attendance was also higher in Emsworth, at 66 per cent, than across the nation as a whole, where the share was barely 50 per cent. From these figures, therefore, it seems clear that Emsworth society as a whole showed a greater propensity to attend church on a Sunday than the nation as a whole, and that the established Anglican Church was still favoured by a majority of churchgoers, with the Baptist

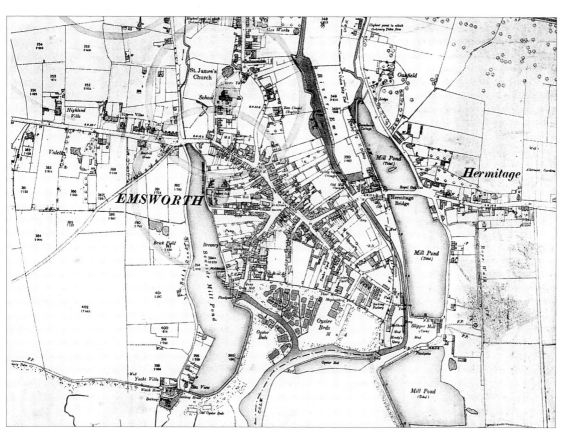

51 *The 1890 O.S. map. A large oyster bed has been created on the mud on the south side of the shipping channel. The King Street industrial area is much as it was in 1870 but a flour mill has been established in the timber yard. This was a steam mill that was operated by Sparks alongside his steam saw mill. The building formerly used as a girls' school in School Lane has become an infants' school. New houses have been built at the northern end of North Street and along Church Road. (Hampshire Record Office)*

Church having the strongest following among the nonconformists. We should not, however, overlook the fact that one third of the town's population seems to have had no contact with organised religion.

Although outwardly a peaceful place, Emsworth witnessed a number of episodes of violent behaviour. Bonfire night celebrations in 1824 were reported as having led to damage to property and injury to passers-by. The night of drunken excess by a small group of men in 1837 which was referred to in Chapter IV also led to damage to property and personal injury. In 1841 the *Hampshire Telegraph*, reporting on an

'Atrocious Outrage at Emsworth', informed its readers that six men had gone to the Sunday evening service at St James's Church with pockets full of fireworks. As the congregation came out, they threw fireworks amongst them and then proceeded to the Square, throwing fireworks on the way. One passer-by was thrown from his gig and knocked unconscious. Such incidents, although rare, alarmed 'respectable' opinion within the town.

Education was one means by which the Church sought to influence the behaviour of the young. In 1841 a large proportion of the children of the town had little or no formal education.

The National School, which in 1839 had moved to a new building in Bridgefoot Path, was too small to accommodate all of the town's children in the 5-13 age group. Fees, albeit nominal, had to be paid and attendance at school was not yet compulsory. The result was that in the 1841 census 272 children in the 5-13 age group were not recorded as being scholars. Amongst the fishing community it was the custom for children to help their parents to supplement the family income. In 1850 the *Hampshire Telegraph* reported that 'in the small rythes on the mud prawns, shrimps, eel, cockles and winkles are caught in abundance, the last two by younger members of the family (who thus easily contribute 4s. or 5s. each to the weekly earnings)'. School places were increased in 1852 with the opening of St James' Church School, adjacent to the new church, although initially this was reserved for boys. Attendance at school was made compulsory by Act of Parliament in 1880, and the 1881 census lists 409 children in the 5-13 age group as scholars, but in this census there were still some 30 children not listed as scholars. Clearly the new law was taking time to be fully enforced, perhaps partly because parents still had to pay fees – the 'weekly pence' – until 1891. Even when schooling finally became a free service attendance at school was still very irregular. The September 1891 edition of the *Emsworth Parish Magazine* expressed the hope that the law granting free education would 'take away any excuse for irregularity of attendance on the ground of not being able to pay the school money'. A year later, however, the magazine was still voicing the same feelings of exasperation. 'As long as a number of parents are so careless about the irregular attendance of the children,' the author wrote, 'the schools never can reach a high standard of efficiency.'

Since 1834 responsibility for the relief of the town's poor had rested with the Havant Poor Law Union. A workhouse had been built in Havant and the affairs of the Union were controlled by an elected Board of Guardians. For many years at the end of the 19th century and the beginning of the 20th century a prominent member, and later chairman, of the Board of Guardians was the leading Emsworth businessman, Albert Tatchell. The aims of the Poor Law Amendment Act of 1834, which grouped parishes into Unions and established workhouses as the main source of relief for the poor, were to drive down the costs of poor relief by deterring the able-bodied poor from applying for it. This was to be achieved by refusing to provide 'paupers' with any financial help and by establishing such a harsh regime in the workhouses that only the genuinely desperate would apply to enter. The minutes of the Havant Poor Law Guardians reveal some of the ways in which this harshness was achieved. In common with all workhouses, families were separated on entering; men, women, boys and girls all occupied separate dormitories. Able-bodied inmates were set to work and in Havant this included the particularly unpleasant task of 'oakum picking'. Inmates were allowed no visitors, except on Tuesdays, and there was a prohibition on the consumption of alcohol, although this rule seems to have been difficult to enforce as there are frequent complaints in the Guardians' minutes that 'the consumption of alcoholic liquor ... has not in any way diminished'. Corporal punishment was also used to discipline the children, although the Guardians did criticise the matron at times for her excessive use of the cane.

The 1881 census shows that of the 96 inmates of the Havant workhouse 18 came from Emsworth. This shows a significant reduction from the 31 persons who were resident in the Emsworth poorhouse in 1814, an indication perhaps that the deterrent nature of the workhouse was having some effect in reducing the numbers who were applying for relief. Of these 18 Emsworth 'paupers', six were children and four were over the age of 70. Amongst the adult male inmates, five were described as labourers, one as a fisherman, one as a mariner and one as a ropemaker. Thus the main causes of poverty were being orphaned,

52 *West Street in the Edwardian era. This view shows a group of people standing on the bridge at the end of the Mill Pond, with Bridgefoot Path to the right.*

53 *North Street in the early 20th century. The butcher's shop belonging to the Silk family is on the right. The only traffic is the horse-drawn vehicles in the background, making it perfectly safe for both the photographer and the children facing the camera to linger in the middle of the road.*

54 *St Peter's Square, possibly late 19th century. The Black Dog Inn, one of the oldest in the town, is on the corner with High Street. The frontages of the shops along this side of the Square have changed little in the past century (see illustration 26, page 34).*

55   *South Street, possibly late 19th century. The Anchor Inn at the foot of South Street was one of the main haunts of the fishermen. In 1878 the inn also became the Customs House for the port.*

having a low-wage occupation or, simply, old age. Seamen and their families were particularly susceptible to periods of hardship. Seamen signed agreements to work on ships for six months at a time and wages were paid at the end of each voyage. Families were left to make ends meet while the main wage earner was away at sea. A round trip to Sunderland and back to fetch a cargo of coal, the type of work most familiar to Emsworth seamen, could last up to a month. Foreign voyages could take seamen away from home for much longer periods. In 1858 the wife of Charles Farndell applied to the Guardians for poor relief when he was away on a two-month trip to Cuba on the vessel *Halifax*. The Guardians' response was to contact the ship's owners in order to secure part of his wages for his wife and family.

Whilst in the workhouse children were sent to school. Once they reached working age the Guardians placed them in employment or training. Some boys were sent to the Royal Navy; others were apprenticed to the fishing industry in Grimsby, to Albert Tatchell's rope and sail factory in Emsworth, or sent to Industrial Schools. Girls were usually placed in service.

The Board of Guardians also had a responsibility for public health within the area. Local doctors were appointed as Medical Officers in each of the parishes within the Union and it was within the Guardians' powers to pay for the medical treatment of poor people within the district. Vaccination against smallpox had been made compulsory under the Vaccination Acts and enforcement was the responsibility of the Boards of Guardians.

In April 1852 the following advertisement appeared in the *Hampshire Telegraph*: 'To be Let, a very commodious FAMILY RESIDENCE … pleasantly situate [sic] in the small and healthy town of Emsworth.' In the following year the Board of Guardians organised a 'house to house visitation' through Emsworth, conducted by the vice-chairman, the Medical Officer, the local

constable and the curate of St James's Church, to identify any 'unhealthy nuisances' which posed a danger to public health. The *Hampshire Telegraph* carried a full report of their investigation:

> It was little expected that so much of unhealthy nuisance existed to justify the necessity of such a careful and impartial search. The practise [sic] of collecting refuse in dry corners and swampy holes for sale as manure is very generally prevalent; ditches, literally the depositories of putrid mud; cess-pools overrunning yards and gardens, in some cases down to the very doors; privies choked and leaking in every direction, all yielding the most noxious and offensive effluvia were abundantly found demanding the most energetic remonstrance … there does exist ample sources of unhealthiness calculated to aggravate any attack from cholera which may … make its appearance.

The Board of Guardians had the power to inspect and to request the removal of the 'nuisances' identified in their visitation but they had no power to compel. Moreover, without an adequate water supply and the provision of mains drainage, most householders were not in a position to make significant improvements to the sanitation of their homes. Most of the poorer Emsworth residents lived in rented homes and improvements were the responsibility of the landlords, not all of whom kept their properties in a satisfactory condition. The Court Books of the Manor of Emsworth record that in 1873 'the copyhold messuages and premises situate in the South Street of Emsworth … which Mary Small now holds … are in a very dilapidated state and the said Mary Small is ordered to put the said premises in a proper state'.

Despite the difficulties, however, some improvements were made. Gas lighting came to the town in 1854. In 1872 the Portsmouth

Water Company was granted permission to supply Emsworth and in the following year iron conduit pipes were laid from Havant to bring a mains water supply to the town. Connection of houses to the mains water supply was, however, expensive, and many of the poorer families still relied on wells and the town pump in the Square until the end of the century. In the 1870s a start was made on laying mains drainage with the construction of two sewers, both of which discharged their untreated sewage directly into the harbour. These improvements, which resulted from the efforts of the Havant Board of Guardians in its capacity as Rural Sanitary Authority, still left Emsworth in an unhealthy state.

In the Victorian period the only alternative for the poor people of the town to the humiliations of the workhouse was self-help. A Friendly Society had been established in Emsworth in 1763 and by 1800 it had about one hundred members. The Annual Meeting of the Friendly Society in 1843 was reported in the press: 100 members marched in procession from the *Anchor Inn* in South Street to St James's Church, preceded by a band. Membership conditions of the society,

however, precluded lower-paid working men from joining. The original members in 1763 each paid two guineas as an entry fee and then 6d. per month. In 1837 the members included many of the local shopkeepers and tradesmen, including John Pratt the chemist, James Hunt, a miller, Richard Collins, a bootmaker and George King, a mariner, but few if any low paid workmen. By 1900, according to Rudkin, there were three Friendly Societies in Emsworth, a Working Men's Benefit Society and a Provident Medical Club. Some of these 'Clubs', as they were also known, were based in public houses. Both the *George Inn* and the *Black Dog* are known to have been associated with medical 'clubs' which paid sickness benefit for a limited period to their members.

Self-help was one means by which thrifty individuals could protect themselves and their families against illness and misfortune. In the 1880s, however, the town had many problems which could only be solved through collective action: poor sanitation, bad housing and the poor state of many of the roads were among the most pressing. These were the challenges that needed to be tackled in the next quarter century.

Make up your own mind with *The Week*

" It represents so many different points of view... I couldn't live without it. "

Alice, London

Opinions are everywhere. Balanced, reliable information is not. That's why our award-winning editorial team collect the best stories from across British and international media every week to give you the full picture. No bias, no fake news — just brilliantly concise editorial.

See for yourself, order your FREE copy.

Over 300,000 readers

Curated from **over 200 news sources**

Condensed, refreshing format

WORTH £3.80

Call 0800 088 2490 today

VII

1890–1914

'The advocates of sanitary improvement'

Writing in the *Parish Magazine* in 1891 the local rector expressed concern about the future development of the town:

> In a quiet little town like Emsworth there is not the scope for all the young people as they grow up, and so they go away, some into service, some to the navy, and others to larger towns … What will be the future of Emsworth is hard to say; the thought seems to be that with increased railroad conveniences it may develop into a kind of residential suburb of Portsmouth.

The combined population of Warblington and Emsworth in 1891 was 2,840. By 1911 the number of people living in the area had grown to 3,771, an increase of over 30 per cent. This pace of expansion was unprecedented in Emsworth's history and was largely the result of inward migration. The town experienced a small-scale building boom in this period. Rows of terraced houses, catering mainly for artisans and lower middle-class families, were built in the Sultan Road, Victoria Road and the Bridge Road areas in the 1890s. Further west along the Havant Road more substantial new housing was developed in Record Road, Park Crescent and Beach Road. In the *Hampshire Telegraph* of June 1901, 97 freehold building plots were offered for sale by auction. This was the Emsworth House estate, which was sold off by its owner, Major

Boyd. The house became a private school, while the land was laid out by William Duffield, a local property developer, as a new housing estate. To the north of the railway line new houses were built in the New Brighton and Horndean Road areas. Much of this new development was the work of William Duffield; in his obituary in the *Hants and Sussex County Press* in June 1918 it was said that 'he was responsible for [Emsworth's] growth from a village to a town'. Apart from stimulating the local building trades and the brick-making industry – the numbers employed in the latter increased from five in 1881 to 11 in 1901 – the building of these new houses attracted into the town many new residents who had been born and were employed elsewhere. The fact that many of the new developments were near to the railway station or to the main road to Havant and Portsmouth suggests that the occupants were treating Emsworth as a place to live rather than to work. The development of Emsworth as a 'residential suburb of Portsmouth' had indeed begun.

Trade directories for this period, however, continued to portray the town in its traditional colours. *Kelly's Directory* of 1895 described Emsworth in the following terms:

> This place is a member of the ports of Portsmouth and Chichester and carries on a trade in the importation of coal and exportation of timber and flour. Several vessels are employed in the coasting trade,

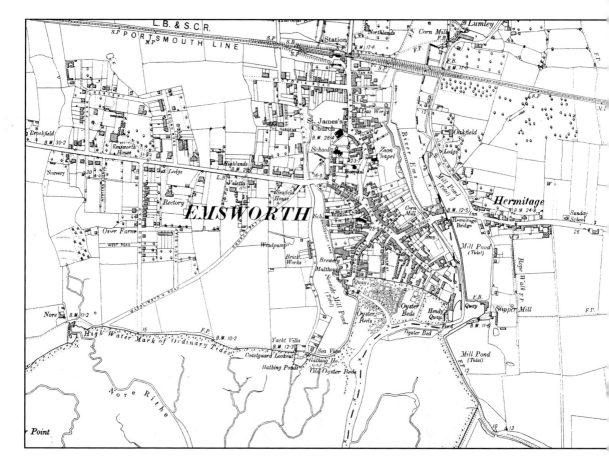

56   *The 1910 O. S. map. The centre of Emsworth and the King Street industrial area has changed little in the 20 years sinc the previous map (see illustration 51). The extensive new housing development to the north and west of the town can clearl be seen. Victoria Road and Sultan Road have become new streets of terraced housing near the railway station. More substantic detached and semi-detached houses have been built in new developments at Record Road, Park Crescent and Beech Roac (Hampshire County Record Office)*

and a considerable number of boats in the oyster industry, for which this town has long been celebrated … The manufacture of sailcloth, sacking, rope and twine and fishing nets is carried on and there are two shipyards and a brewery.

These traditional trades were experiencing mixed fortunes as the 19th century drew to a close. The port was still very busy in the mid-1890s. At a public inquiry into proposed improvements to the harbour, held in 1896, its was stated that 129 vessels with a combined tonnage of 5,264 tons

had called at the port in 1895. To the regula shipments of coal were added those of sand, grave and bricks for the building boom, which were brought in through the port, together with load of manure for local farmers. In addition, there had been 148 separate dockings by oyster smacks William Foster, coal merchant, ship owner and shipbuilder, showed renewed confidence in the coastal trade in coal in the 1890s. He had a new vessel, the *Fortuna*, built in 1892 and bought back the *Isabella* in 1898. The revival, however, wa short-lived. The *Fortuna* was sold to a Scottish owner in 1901, and in the remaining year

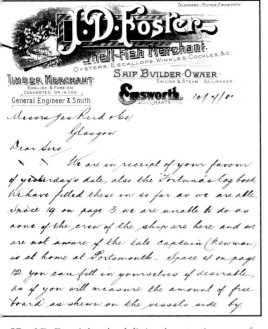

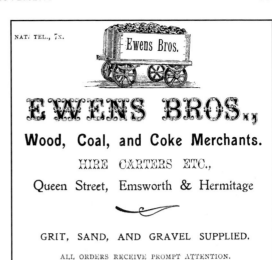

58 *A 1912 advertisement for Ewens Brothers. As coal and timber merchants, Ewens were one of the main local competitors for Foster and Co. The picture of a railway goods wagon confirms that railways had become the main means of bringing coal into the town.*

57 *J.D. Foster's letterhead, listing the extensive range of business activities carried on by this company. This letter refers to the sale of the* Fortuna *in 1901 to James Reid and Co. of Glasgow. (Portsmouth City Record Office)*

59 *The Emsworth shipyard. This late 19th-century view shows the slipway down which vessels were launched. A recently launched barge is being fitted out on the foreshore whilst another completed barge is at anchor in the harbour.*

before the outbreak of war very few vessels were involved in bringing regular cargoes of coal into Emsworth. In the 1890s W. Foster began acquiring a fleet of coal wagons and more wagons were purchased in the early years of the 20th century. By 1914 Foster was receiving deliveries of coal via various railway companies from Yorkshire, Nottinghamshire and South Wales. Not all of these wagons were delivered to Emsworth station. Serving a wide area in south-east Hampshire and West Sussex, Foster had wagons delivered to Havant, Rowlands Castle, Bosham, Singleton and Selham. By 1914 the bulk of the coal purchased by Foster and other Emsworth coal merchants was brought in by rail.

Emsworth's two shipyards were kept busy throughout the 1890s. J.D. Foster's yard completed at least 10 fishing vessels, a steam tug and a large, floating oyster storage crate in the years 1890-1902. The *Fortuna* appears to have been the last large brig built in the Emsworth shipyard of Apps, and in the 1890s the main work of the shipyard was the building of barges. The *County Press* of April 1896 reported that 'another large barge has been launched from the Apps shipyard'. These were vessels of about 20-30 tons displacement which were mainly used for the collection and

61 *Another sailing barge anchored near the Town Quay. This photograph, probably taken in the 1920s, also shows the brewery in the background.*

carriage of sand and gravel dredged up from the harbour bottom. The building of a number of these vessels at this time reflects the growth in demand for construction materials that had arisen from the increase in house building.

Shipments of flour to London had all but ceased by the end of the century. The last recorded voyage by a vessel carrying grain or flour to London was made by the *Champion* in 1880. The shipping records show that there were three other small sailing vessels engaged in the corn trade through Emsworth at the turn of the century. The *Hester*, owned by J. Matthews of Emsworth, was described as 'employed in the corn trade between ports in the Solent', with occasional visits to Emsworth. The *Exchange*, owned by Dittman and Malpass, was trading between Chichester Harbour ports and Southampton between 1904 and 1913. The *Emsworth* was also carrying corn meal between Emsworth, the Isle of Wight and Southampton. The output of the local mills, therefore, was once again serving a mainly local market. Nevertheless, trade was sufficiently buoyant to justify the expense of modernising

60 *The* Exchange *unloading at the Town Quay. This vessel was one of the barges engaged in the corn trade with other local ports. In the foreground is the small steam tug, the* Dora, *which is being used here for a family outing.*

62   A view of the harbour, c.1910. The large wooden structure in the centre right of the picture is the Ark. Much of Foster's fishing fleet is at anchor in the harbour. The vessel tied up next to the Ark is the so-called Echo II, *which was completed in 1903 but never put to sea. The* Echo *can be seen to the left of the Ark in mid-channel.*

the mills. After being completely destroyed by fire in 1894, the Town Mill was rebuilt with a water turbine to replace the old wheel. According to *Kelly's Directory* it was also equipped with a steam engine to provide auxiliary power. By the turn of the century the Quay Mill and Lumley Mill had also been fitted with auxiliary steam engines.

The oyster fishing industry experienced remarkable growth during the 1890s. By the turn of the century 100,000 oysters were passing through Emsworth each week, and the oyster fishing fleet of J.D. Foster was one of the most highly developed fleets in the country. Between 1890 and 1901 Foster's own shipbuilding yard constructed a further seven fishing vessels to add to the four that had already been completed since 1888. The yard also built a steam tug, the *Dora,* in 1895, and in 1898 the so-called 'Ark'. This was a gigantic crate with large openings around the sides and open at the top, which was designed to be moored in the harbour and used for the unloading and sorting of oysters and scallops. The experiment proved to be a

costly failure. The Ark was never used and was left stranded on the mud in the harbour to rot slowly away.

The failure of the Ark notwithstanding, Foster built up a highly successful oyster fishing business. The designs of his vessels were innovatory in many respects. His four larger smacks – *Evolution, Nonpareil, Sylvia* and *Echo* – were all fitted with steam winches to help with the sails and hauling in the dredges. Each ship had a well built into it amidships and a system of pipes and pumps that enabled a constant supply of fresh seawater to be circulated through the well to keep the catch fresh. Scoops on the *Echo* were arranged in such a way that seawater could be directed into the well while the ship was under way. The *Echo* also had an auxiliary steam engine to provide additional power, particularly in calm conditions. Foster's vessels also had very graceful lines. With their clipper bows, slim lines and raked sterns, J. Reger considered them 'the finest working fishing craft ever built in English ports'.

Oyster fishing was carried on during the autumn, winter and early spring. Fishing smacks from Emsworth would join those from other ports around the south and east coasts in dredging for oysters off Shoreham, across the Channel between the Isle of Wight and Cherbourg, and off the Dutch coast. There was also fishing for

63   Emsworth harbour in the Edwardian period. A collection of small fishing boats (jerkies) has been been moored alongside the sea wall. Larger fishing smacks belonging to Foster are visible in the background.

64 *The Quay Mill, with fishing boats tied up at the sea wall. This photograph provides a clear view of the traditional lines of the jerkies, the vessels used by the independent local fishermen.*

escallops, mainly off Beachy Head. Escallop fishing, which was primarily undertaken in the months of December through to April, was more popular among the crews because the rewards were greater. Crews on the fishing vessels were small. Under James Cribb's ownership the small fishing smack *Jane* had carried a crew of six or seven. After Foster bought the vessel he reduced the crew to just three. On the larger vessels that were built in the 1890s the normal complement was six men for the cutters and eight for the ketches. Another innovation introduced by Foster was to bring in ships' masters and crew from other oyster fishing ports, utilising their experience in sailing the larger vessels. The crew of the *Thistle* in 1889 included three men from Brightlingsea in Essex whilst, in 1897, the *Sylvia* was commanded by a Brightlingsea man and had four Emsworth men in a crew of seven. Crews were paid a share of the catch and Foster had a reputation among the fishermen for paying the crew a smaller share than other ship owners. According to Amos Boutell, a ship's master who gave evidence against Foster at a legal hearing in 1906, many Emsworth men refused to sail on the *Echo* because they could not get sufficient pay for their work.

Although Emsworth was the home port for Foster's vessels, it became normal practice for them to unload some of their catches in the port of Newhaven. Foster also began to buy in young oysters – the 'spat' – from oyster merchants in Whitstable and elsewhere for laying down and maturing in the Emsworth oyster beds. His business was a far cry from the small-scale inshore fishing in family-owned 'jerkies' that was still practised by the more traditional Emsworth fishermen.

John (Jack) Kennett was the other main figure in the Emsworth fishing industry by the end of the century. His vessels were much smaller than those of Foster, as was the size of his business. He owned two ketches, the *Guide* and the *Gipsy*

65 *Emsworth harbour, c.1898. The shipyard is just visible on the right of the picture. Vessels belonging to Foster's fishing fleet are at anchor in the harbour.*

Queen, together with a smaller fishing smack, the *Tim Whiffler*. He also owned two barges which were used for his sand and gravel business, the *May* and the *Topsy*. As President of the Emsworth Dredgermen's Co-operative Society, Jack Kennett was closer than Foster to the small independent fishermen of the town.

By the early 1890s many of the townspeople were beginning to voice their frustrations at the slow pace of improvement in the town and their feeling that the Havant Local Board of Health was too remote from Emsworth to give the town the attention it needed. At a meeting held in February 1893 a group of local residents led by Joshua Mosdell, an auctioneer, Mr Forder, Mr Hales and Mr Coffin presented the case for Emsworth to have its own Local Board (Town Council). Despite opposition from leading figures in the Warblington parish, including the Reverend Buller Norris and Major Boyd J.P., the proposal was backed by the majority of those present. A local poll was held in April 1893 and the result was a majority of more than two to one in favour of an Emsworth Local Board. The promoters of the reform organised a vigorous and effective campaign under the banners 'Cast off the Bondage of Havant', 'Let Emsworth spend its own money', and 'Be Loyal to your Town and Parish and Vote for the Local Board'. The argument was won but reform of local government in Emsworth was delayed until the government had introduced a national reform. In 1895 the Warblington Urban District Council was established. With its offices in Emsworth, and most of its work concerned with addressing the long-neglected needs of the town, the WUDC was often referred to as the Emsworth Town Council, but its official title reflected the traditional precedence of Warblington over Emsworth.

The new council consisted of 12 members elected by the ratepayers of the district. As rate-paying was linked to property ownership the franchise in local government elections was relatively restricted. The 1892 electoral roll for the Warblington division of Hampshire County Council contained only 375 names out of a total population of over 2,000 people. Of these, however, 64 were women, since in local government elections, if not yet in parliamentary elections, women could qualify to vote on the same terms as men. Because of the restricted franchise it is not surprising that the majority of those elected to the WUDC, and to the Poor Law Guardians, was drawn exclusively from the local

66 *Emsworth harbour from the sea wall, c.1910. The Ark is clearly visible in this photograph. The large fishing ketch in the middle distance is the* Gipsy Queen *which belonged to Jack Kennett.*

67 *The council offices. This building in North Street was constructed in 1900 to house the offices of the new Warblington Urban District Council. The office of the Sanitary Inspector is on the ground floor to the left of the building; the Fire Station is on the right. Today the upper floor of this building is occupied by the Emsworth Museum. (EMHT/Privett)*

gentry, the clergy and the business community. The 12 members of the WUDC included J.D. Foster, Albert Tatchell, Jack Kennett, Joshua Mosdell, Mr Kinnell, Mr Mant and Mr Duffield, all local businessmen. In his election address for 1910 Duffield expressed his belief that 'businessmen with peaceful minds … should run and keep

68   *Emsworth's volunteer firemen proudly parade with their new motor appliance (c. 1920s). Previously the local fire brigade had operated a horse-drawn appliance.*

our town'. The clergy were represented by the Reverend H.G. Sprigg. Albert Tatchell and Joshua Mosdell were also members of the Havant Union Board of Guardians where they worked alongside Major Boyd J.P., Lieut-Gen. Sir F. Fitzwygram and two clergymen. Working men were yet to make any impact on local affairs. Women, however, were slowly beginning to make their presence felt. By 1911 there was an elected female member of the Poor Law Guardians, Miss Hodgkinson, and two co-opted members of Guardians' committees, including Miss Jewell of Emsworth.

Elections in the early years of the UDC were not fought on political lines. Candidates stressed their commitment to low rates and opposition to unnecessary expenditure and most declared themselves to be independents. After 1910, however, political parties began to organise more openly in the town, with the Conservatives leading the way. An Emsworth and Havant Unionist Association was founded in 1910, with Dr Lockhart Stephens as its Chairman and Albert Tatchell as Honorary Treasurer. There was also an active local branch of the Primrose League, a body closely linked to the Conservative and Unionist Party. Liberal strength is much harder to gauge, although the presence of many nonconformists

within the town provided some potential for Liberal support.

The new council had much work to do. The promoters of an Emsworth Local Board had argued that the sanitary condition of the town had long been neglected, with many houses not connected to the mains drainage and many cesspits in an appalling condition. The *County Press*, in an editorial on the occasion of an election for the UDC in 1896, advised its readers to 'plump for the advocates of sanitary improvement'. Two miles of roads within the district, which had not been adopted by the Havant authority, were in urgent need of repair. One of the first acts of the new council was to extend the sewerage system in the town. Two new drains were laid and were connected to the existing sewers, thereby increasing the discharge of raw sewage into the harbour. The council appointed a Medical Officer of Health, Dr Lockhart Stephens, a surveyor and a harbour master. In 1900 new premises were opened in North Street and a new fire engine was acquired.

In 1896 the council began moves to take over control of the harbour. Navigation in the harbour had not been subject to any legal controls previously. There had been an unofficial rrangement among the local merchants and harbour users to pay voluntary tolls to a committee ppointed by themselves. The money raised was upposed to be used to provide proper markings or the navigation channels, but the voluntary rrangements had broken down in 1894 amidst much criticism of J.D. Foster. He had been esponsible for collecting the fees but no proper ccounts had been kept and the markings of the hannels by means of posts and buoys had been neglected. The final straw for other harbour users had been Foster's unilateral establishment of new oyster beds in one of the channels. The new ouncil proposed to constitute itself as a Harbour Authority with a view to making improvements o the harbour, such as building new wharves, traightening the channel and installing new navigation markers. All of this would be funded by the collection of tolls from harbour users. The council's case was that trade was declining because vessels were often being stranded on the mud and the larger vessels could not enter or eave the port safely. The scheme was approved by the Board of Trade and the council duly gained control over the harbour.

The Fosters were the most vocal and consistent opponents of the council's efforts to egulate and improve the harbour. Arguing that he plan would interfere with fishing, drive trade away and be very expensive to implement, they voiced their opposition both from within the council chamber and at public meetings. They were supported in their opposition by Joshua Mosdell, who voiced the ratepayers' concerns about expenditure out of the public purse, but opposed by Jack Kennett and Albert Tatchell, both of whom had a direct interest in the harbour and shipping. The council, unsure of its powers and of the extent of popular support for its plans, took no action for some years. Meanwhile, J.D. Foster continued to behave in a high-handed manner. When his large oyster storage crate, the Ark, proved to be a failure he abandoned it on a mud bank in the harbour, posing an additional hazard

to shipping. Finally, in 1902, the council attempted to act against him. He was ordered to remove his 'hulk' or pay the costs if the council had to do it. He ignored the order. The Harbour Master also considered that the mud bank protecting Foster's new oyster bed on the Thorney side of the channel was a hazard to shipping. When he refused to remove it, in November 1902, the Harbour Master, Council Surveyor and a contractor went onto the mud at low tide and attempted to remove it themselves. A group of fishermen employed by Foster obstructed the operation, with Foster as an interested bystander, and the council team withdrew. No further attempts were made to force Foster to remove the obstacles. The council had been advised that it had the legal power to take action against Foster but the costs of such action, on an issue which did not have the unanimous support of the members of the council, persuaded it to allow the issue to rest. Foster had won this particular trial of strength and the harbour improvements were quietly forgotten. The Harbour Master resigned and does not appear to have been replaced.

The annual reports by the Medical Officer began to provide firm evidence of the insanitary and unhealthy condition of some parts of the town. In one of his first reports, in 1897, Dr Stephens sounded an optimistic note about the health of the town. 'The death rate in this district is extremely low,' he reported, going on to say that 'two new sewers have been laid and it is considered that the needs of the town are now provided for.' Deaths from infectious diseases, however, soon prompted a change in the tone of his reports. There had been eight deaths from typhoid in 1897; this figure increased to 10 in 1899, 17 in 1901 and peaked at 22 in 1902. There were also several deaths each year from diphtheria, scarlatina and bronchitis, and many of the victims were children under the age of five. The Log Book of the Council School recorded many occasions in these years when the school was affected by outbreaks of diphtheria, scarlet fever and whooping cough, which occasionally necessitated closing the school for a period. Dr Stephens was able through his work to identify the sources of the outbreaks of disease, particularly typhoid. 'Typhoid fever,' he wrote in 1902, 'has for many years been considered endemic in this district ... Where sewerage is imperfect, or where leaky cesspits exist, there typhoid is prone to occur.' Two years earlier he had been more specific:

> With regard to the locality of infectious disease it was found that most cases occur where there were sanitary defects, the worst of which by far are the stinking privy pits at so many of the poorer cottages in Emsworth, especially in Nile Street, South Street and Queen Street.

He also highlighted the need for better housing. Some of the cottages in 'the older part of the town,' he wrote in 1910, 'come very near to the designation of insanitary dwellings.' He was a champion of the cause of providing good cheap accommodation for working people:

> There is room for more good cottage property in the district at reasonable rents, the majority of cottages erected in recent years being rented somewhat higher than the average working man can afford. Working men want good, well constructed cottages, not villas.

Those sewers which had been built in Emsworth discharged raw sewage directly into the harbour near the oyster beds, and the inevitable problems resulting from this were being noted by 1900. J.D. Foster wrote to the Board of Trade in 1896 complaining that 'the Council propose to injure the fishing industry by discharging directly into the harbour, to the detriment of the fish', but the council had replied that 'no discharge detrimental to sea fishing exists in their district'. In 1900 the Portsmouth Medical Officer was reported as claiming that 'nearly half the deaths from typhoid fever in Portsmouth were the result

of eating these [Emsworth] cockles'. Later that year it was reported that two deaths from typhoid in Cosham had been traced back to the eating of Emsworth cockles.

The council had begun to address the issue and by 1900 was considering a scheme for building new sewers and a sewage treatment works at a cost of between 12 and 15 thousand pounds. The first obstacle to be overcome was opposition from ratepayers, always vocal when large amounts of expenditure were proposed. At a ratepayers' meeting in October 1900 one of the elected councillors, Joshua Mosdell, was the leading opponent of a new main drainage scheme on the grounds of cost. Secondly, the council's decision-making procedures did not lend themselves to quick and decisive action. Many times the issue was discussed by the council, only for a decision to be deferred, and by 1902 nothing more had been done to improve the situation. In November of that year Emsworth oysters were served at a banquet in Winchester, several guests became ill and the Dean of Winchester died. The death of such a prominent person finally led to action being taken. In January 1903 the Medical Officer banned the sale of Emsworth oysters, an action which led J.D. Foster to sue the council for damages of £18,000 and to halt the building of a new vessel. Foster claimed at the time that in the week before Christmas he would normally sell about 100,000 oysters, but because of the adverse publicity and the subsequent ban his sales had dwindled to virtually nothing: 'I have at present in the beds about half a million oysters, valued at between £1,000 and £2,000 but they cannot be sold.'

There was also considerable hardship for the local fishermen and their families. According to the *County Press* there were between 200 and 300 inhabitants of Emsworth who were dependent on oyster fishing during the winter months. In February 1903 it was reported that many of them were having to pawn their clothes to raise money for food.

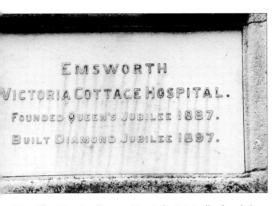

69　*The Victoria Cottage Hospital. Originally founded in King Street in 1887 to mark the Queen's Golden Jubilee, the Cottage Hospital moved to its present site in North Street in 1897. This foundation stone marks the occasion.*

The legal case, which dragged on for over three years, divided the local community. Jack Kennett, like Foster an oyster merchant and member of the council, gave evidence on the council's behalf when the case finally reached court. Kennett told the court that the decline in the oyster trade had been only temporary and that sales had begun to pick up in the 1903 season. His three vessels had continued to work at full capacity, as had those of Foster. Although the sale of oysters from the Emsworth beds was banned, the ships could still dredge for oysters and escallops in the Channel and land their catches at other ports such as Newhaven. The price of oysters had fallen because of the scare but merchants such as Kennett and Foster had protected their profits by cutting the payments made to the fishermen. The court found that the council was liable for the damage caused to the oyster trade but, in the light of Kennett's evidence, Foster was awarded only nominal damages of £850. The council's legal costs, however, were high and necessitated the imposition of a special five-shilling rate to meet the bill.

With the legal case settled the sewerage scheme could finally proceed, but it was not until 1910 that the council finally secured approval from the Local Government Board for raising the loan that was needed to finance it. The new sewage treatment works was finally opened in 1914. Meanwhile, Jack Kennett's contribution to saving the council and ratepayers from costly compensation was marked by the presentation to him of a gold watch paid for by public subscription.

Despite the delay, the deaths from infectious disease in Emsworth had been steadily falling since 1902. There were 12 deaths from typhoid in 1904, two in 1906 and none at all in 1908. Deaths from other infectious diseases were also in decline. On the other hand, cases of infectious diseases were still being reported; there were seven cases of typhoid in 1914, 12 of scarlatina and 13 of diphtheria. The reduction in typhoid cases was probably due to the ban on eating local shellfish, together with the efforts of the council and Dr Stephens to ensure that cesspits were emptied more regularly. Emsworth still had unhealthy districts in 1914, but the situation was slowly beginning to improve.

Care of the sick in the town had been improving since 1888, when the Emsworth Jubilee Cottage Hospital had been founded in King Street. In 1897, to mark Queen Victoria's Diamond Jubilee, a larger hospital was opened

70　*The Victoria Cottage Hospital in the Edwardian period. The council yard, with a variety of appliances, can be seen behind the hospital. (EMHT/Privett)*

71 *An Emsworth regatta in the Edwardian period. Pleasure sailing was becoming an increasingly popular activity in Emsworth. The race shown here appears to be one for 'bona fide fishing boats'.*

in North Street. This was run by a charitable trust and the treatment of patients could only be funded by subscriptions and fees. The trustees extolled the virtues of self-help in justifying the charging of fees for treatment:

> The fee encourages thrift and manly independence and is welcomed by the honest working man who, whilst ready to accept the help that is necessary, is perfectly willing to do what he can for his own support.

72 *The Emsworth Regatta, 1910. There were attempts to make the Regatta an annual event in the pre-war years. In this picture a large yacht can be seen in the background. The presence of a number of Royal Navy sailors in the rowing boat in the foreground reflects the fact that many young men from Emsworth had joined the senior service.*

The hospital was supported by an annual subscription from the Poor Law Guardians, and those who qualified for poor relief were able to get free treatment at the hospital, but all other patients were expected to pay for it.

There was another Emsworth which existed alongside the traditional fishing and trading part of the town. Since the early 19th century the number of 'private residents' listed in the directories had been steadily increasing and more of the larger villa-style detached homes had been built to accommodate them. Emsworth appears to have been a particularly attractive place for former naval officers to settle in on their retirement. The sheltered harbour was of particular interest to yachting enthusiasts and *Kelly's Directory* of 1895 reported that 'of late years this place has acquired popularity as a yachting station, especially for the laying up of yachts in the winter.' Similarly, in March 1893, the *Hampshire Telegraph* commented that 'there are now nearly a score of yachts in the harbour, including the *Tsar*, a schooner of 145 tons, and the *Maid of Scurr*, 40 tons'.

Many of the local fishermen, unable to dredge for oysters in the summer months, took employment on the larger yachts. Amos Boutell for example, served on the German Kaiser's

73 *P.G. Wodehouse or 'Plum' as he was affectionately known, came to live in Emsworth in 1903. This photograph shows him as a young man aged 20, and was taken just prior to his time in Emsworth.*

yacht, *Meteor*, and in 1903 he was employed as quartermaster on the yacht *Sybarite* when it was racing in America. Charles Wells served on the royal racing yacht in the reign of Edward VII and also on Lord Brassey's yacht, *Sunbeam*. The skills of seamanship which they had learned on the Emsworth fishing smacks were clearly highly regarded by the wealthy owners of the racing yachts.

Regattas had been held in Emsworth harbour as early as the 1870s. An Emsworth Boating Club held its first dinner in 1888, and in 1894 an Emsworth Corinthians Sailing Club held a week-long water carnival. There were regattas in each of the following two years, after which the club appears to have collapsed. The regatta was revived in 1900 and there were intermittent events in the years 1900-14, including a Boxing Day regatta in 1910. Not all of the races in these

regattas were for recreational sailors; there were races too for '*bona fide* fishing boats', in which local fishermen such as the Parham and Prior families participated, and Harry Prior – known locally as 'the Admiral' – was a member of the Regatta Committee.

A number of small private schools was established in Emsworth to educate the children of these well-to-do families. Emsworth House School, a preparatory boarding school for boys, was established by Baldwin King-Hall in 1901 after the Emsworth House estate was sold for new building development. Described as a 'rather eccentric but efficient and happy establishment', the school also became a country retreat for the young P.G. Wodehouse, who was beginning to make his way in the world as a full-time writer. Through his friendship with Herbert Westbrook, a master, Wodehouse came to live and help at the school in 1903. Although not himself a schoolmaster, he was actively involved in the life of the school in a number of ways. He helped Ella King-Hall, the sister of the proprietor, to produce plays and musicals. On Sports Days he could be found acting as a judge and he was a regular member of the school's cricket team. In 1904 Wodehouse moved into the house called Threepwood in the new development of Record Road and he continued to live there, supported by his housekeeper Lilian, for the next ten years. During those years his literary output was prodigious. In addition to writing his weekly newspaper column, 'By the Way', he also produced during his Emsworth years no fewer than 18 books and seven plays. His work involved him in frequent visits to London – so frequent in fact that from 1907 he rented a flat in the capital – and also, from 1909, he made regular visits to the USA. With an increasingly busy and hectic schedule, Wodehouse found in Emsworth the peace and quiet he needed to concentrate on his writing.

Wodehouse immortalised the name of the town through his character, Lord Emsworth. The many other references to local people and places in his books indicate that he drew inspiration from the area. Freddy Threepwood, Felix Clovelly and Lord Mount Anville are all names drawn from houses in Record Road. Colonel Arthur Mant was a reference to William Mant, a prominent local shopkeeper with whom Wodehouse had an account. The names of Lady Ann Warblington, Lord Bosham, the Duchess of Havant and the Countess of Southbourne are all taken from places in the Emsworth area which Wodehouse probably would have visited on his cycling expeditions. He appears to have been more an observer of rather than an active participant in the social life of the town although he did become something of a local celebrity, at least in the view of the town's newspaper, for his prowess as a cricketer. His performance in a match in October 1910 when he took four wickets and scored 38 runs earned him the soubriquet, in the match report, of the 'little giant'. On another occasion, in July 1914, he was singled out for praise by the match reporter in the following glowing terms: 'Hitting brilliantly all around the wicket, Wodehouse reached fifty in half an hour.' Wodehouse gave up his lease on Threepwood in 1915 and his Emsworth years came to an end. Although he made some visits to Emsworth House in the 1920s he never again lived in the town. Nevertheless, the time he spent there left its impression both on him and on local people.

Events such as the Diamond Jubilee of Queen Victoria and the coronations of Edward VII in 1902 and of George V in 1911 gave local people opportunities to express their patriotism. The 1902 coronation was marked by a day of celebrations, which included a procession from the Square to the common, accompanied by the Emsworth Town Brass Band and the National School's Fife and Drum Band. An afternoon of sports was followed by a tea, and the day ended with fireworks and a bonfire. Free beer was provided by Kinnell and Hartley, the local brewer. The Boer War, from 1899 to 1902, also gave rise to

74 *Adverts for local businesses, 1912. The Mant family had a number of business interests and William Mant was a holder of several local council offices.*

many expressions of patriotism, especially the celebrations which greeted the relief of Mafeking in May 1900. The town was decked out in flags, a half-day holiday was proclaimed and there was a hastily arranged procession through the town in the evening. Processions of a different kind, however, marred the celebrations for the relief of Ladysmith in March 1900. On that occasion there were two nights of disturbances when large crowds of young men, reportedly 500 strong, had marched around the streets banging tin cans and trays, singing patriotic songs, and breaking the windows of any residents they suspected of having 'pro-Boer' sympathies. Two local shoemakers

75 *A display of patriotic bunting in North Street. The occasion for this was the coronation of George V in 1911. The traction engine is believed to have belonged to the local brewery.*

76 *Emsworth Carnival, 1909. A group of children in fancy dress is waiting in Bath Road for the carnival procession to begin.*

77 *Emsworth Sports, 1913. The caption reads 'The policemen and the suffragette'. On these occasions fancy dress was not solely the preserve of children. (EMHT/Hudson)*

78 *Adverts for local businesses, 1912. Rubick's shoemaking business, which had been in Emsworth for generations, was still able to offer locally made boots and shoes.*

Cooper and Sheerman, were among the victims. Such incidents, however, were rare.

The period 1890 to 1914 saw many changes in Emsworth. The town had grown rapidly, with many new housing developments. Local self-government had finally been granted to the area in 1895 and the new council had begun to make some impact on the state of the roads, the sanitation and the health of the town. Despite setbacks such as the oyster scare of 1902, most businesses in the town were still flourishing and succeeding in adapting to changing conditions. Although the quays in the harbour were less busy in 1914 than they had been a quarter of a century before, the sea still played a vital role in shaping and defining the town.

VIII

1914–1939

'The big boats have practically left us altogether'

The United Kingdom entered the Great War on 3 August 1914. As the country embarked on the greatest conflict in its history young men from the Emsworth district rushed to enlist. Those who were already reservists, such as the members of the Emsworth Territorial Association, were recalled to the colours in the early days of the war. By November, according to the *Hampshire Telegraph,* some 36 officers and over 180 men from other ranks in the district had enlisted in the Royal Navy, and about twenty officers and 160 other men had joined the Army. The maritime connections of Emsworth are clearly reflected in the larger numbers who joined the Royal Navy. Over the coming months and years the numbers joining the forces continued to grow, especially after the introduction of conscription in 1916. The removal of the majority of young men from the local community had far-reaching repercussions.

Although Mr Asquith's government adopted a policy of 'business as usual' in the early months of the conflict, the war brought severe disruption to many aspects of the life of the town. As early as the beginning of September 1914 the local football club had to abandon all of its matches because 19 of its regular players were by then serving in the forces. Fishing was one of the first local industries to feel the effects of wartime restrictions. Fishermen were prohibited from moving over their best fishing grounds between sunset and sunrise, the best hours for catching fish, and all fishing in the harbour required a permit from the authorities. During the war years there were some prosecutions of fishermen by the police for breaking these regulations. With so many of the younger fishermen away in the Royal Navy, fishing in wartime became an occupation for older men and young boys. There were reports as early as September 1914 of distress among the fishing families.

During the first week of the war local businesses were visited by military officers who 'commandeered some of the best horses in the district'. The *County Press* reported that 'they were horses of the heavy type and we understand animals have been taken from the stables of Messrs Silver, Foster, Tier, Ewens Bros and the Council'. Many of the firms affected were the coal merchants who were also finding it increasingly difficult to obtain supplies. The seaborne trade in coal did continue during the war but with increasing difficulty. Later in August 1914 the *County Press* reported on the arrival of a coal brig from the north east: 'Mr Divers arrived at Emsworth on Tuesday on his well known ship, the *Union,* having run the gauntlet down the North Sea from Newcastle with a cargo of coal.' The dangers of trying to continue with normal trade during wartime were underlined in 1916 when the *Fortuna,* once owned by W. Foster, was sunk by a German U-boat off Portland Bill.

Some local businesses clearly benefited from the war. One such was the firm of Carter, Sons and Lewis (formerly Tatchell's), makers and suppliers of rope, twine, sacks and canvas. The company's records show occasional orders from military establishments such as the Portsmouth Dockyard in November 1914, which purchased oakum (tarred rope), and the Ordnance Depot at Hilsea in 1917. There was also an order for canvas from Wells Aviation in 1917, presumably for covering the wings and fuselages of aircraft. But the main business of the firm during the war was with local farmers. As agriculture boomed so too did the businesses of agricultural suppliers. Asking for (and being granted) exemption from military service in 1916, a local ropemaker argued that 'since the war [his] trade had been swamped

and it was absolutely impossible to get the men' Between 1914 and 1918 the takings of this firm more than doubled. Even allowing for wartime inflation, this represents a very substantial increase in business. Meanwhile J.D. Foster, forced to lay up his fishing vessels for the duration of the war branched out into farming. By the end of the war he owned three farms.

In some cases women workers began to fill the gaps left by male employees who had left to serve in the forces. Female porters were employed at the railway station. The Town Mill, which became involved in the production of plywood components for the Sopwith aircraft being built at Chidham, employed women machinists.

Lighting restrictions were introduced in the autumn of 1914. Gas lamps were painted black

79 *John Lewis House. Now converted to a private dwelling, this building in King Street was the sail and ropemaking factory of the Tatchell family and, later, John Lewis and Co. The hoist above the central archway and the arch giving access to a loading area are the visible signs that this was once an industrial building.*

on the tops and sides, shops were prohibited from burning outside lamps or window lamps, and such was the effect of these restrictions that the *Hampshire Telegraph* reported in October 1914 that 'some parts of the town are in perfect darkness'. The only occasion during the war when these lighting restrictions might have been necessary, however, was in September 1916, when a Zeppelin airship passed over the town after a bombing raid on Portsmouth. Other restrictions were also imposed. In October 1914 public houses were ordered to close at 9 p.m., and in October 1916 local shopkeepers agreed to close earlier in the evening, at 7 p.m.

Those who were not eligible to serve in the forces could show their support for the war effort in a number of ways. In August 1914 the Warblington UDC set up a committee to collect funds for the Prince of Wales National Relief Fund, established to relieve financial distress caused by the war. Through house-to-house collections and other fund-raising efforts the collection had raised £175 by October. It was proposed that local fishing families should receive help from the National Relief Fund. A Belgian Relief Fund had also been established to support Belgian refugees who had fled the advance of the German army in the early weeks of the war. Through jumble sales and a fund-raising concert the Belgian Relief

Fund locally raised over £100 by the end of October.

In December 1914 a Red Cross hospital was established at Northlands on the northern side of Emsworth. This former private residence with its large rooms was converted into a small hospital, complete with an operating theatre and 25 beds. By Christmas the first wounded had arrived and were receiving treatment, including six Belgian soldiers. Voluntary donations by local people made an important contribution to the work of the hospital. The war offered many opportunities for voluntary work in support of the war effort, which were enthusiastically embraced. In October 1915 a War Hospital Supply Depot was opened in a house provided by William Duffield. Drawing upon the needleworking skills of local women and carpentry skills of the men, the depot made and supplied bandages, surgical dressings, bed tables and so on to hospitals for the wounded. By November 1916 it was able to call upon 341 local people to do this work. A War Weapons Week was held in June 1918 with the aim of raising £5,000 to pay for three aeroplanes, one of which was to be named 'Emsworth'. By the end of the week £18,000 had been raised.

In January 1916 the voluntary principle in military recruitment was abandoned and conscription was introduced. A Military Tribunal

80 *Northlands. Used as a Red Cross hospital for war casualties in the First World War, Northlands later became a maternity home. It is shown here in a dilapidated state prior to its demolition in the 1970s, to make way for the new A27 trunk road.*

was established in Emsworth to hear cases brought by men applying for exemption from military service. It consisted of four councillors from the UDC, a military officer and two representatives of labour. During the next two years the Tribunal was kept busy hearing appeals from local men. Hardly any of these appeals were made on the basis of conscientious objection to the war; most were from men who argued that their work was of national importance and were supported by their employers, who claimed that the men could not easily be replaced. On this basis the Tribunal gave exemptions, sometimes on a temporary basis, to the ropemaker already mentioned, to some fishermen, the manager of the gasworks and the stoker employed at the gasworks. Most appeals, however, were unsuccessful.

In 1918 American soldiers began to build an aerodrome at nearby Southbourne. A committee was formed in Emsworth to welcome the Americans and raise money to provide social facilities for soldiers in the town. As a result of these efforts, in October a Welcome Club was established at a house in Queen Street. Called the Chevron Club, it was open to American NCOs in their off-duty time. The committee also organised a dance in the Town Hall for the rank and file soldiers. Giving thanks for these efforts, an American officer said, 'As citizen soldiers of the USA we take off our hats to each and all of the people of Emsworth.'

Hardly had the Chevron Club been opened when the war came to an end. News of the Armistice on 11 November 1918 was brought to Emsworth in the early morning by a sailor who had cycled over from Portsmouth. During the day special thanksgiving services were held in local churches, flags and bunting were quickly displayed, and the US Army band marched over from Southbourne to play music in the Square. Within two weeks the Americans were preparing to return home and the town was beginning to adjust to the return of peace. Sadly, however, 100 men from Emsworth did not return.

PEACE CELEBRATIONS
SATURDAY 19TH JULY, 1919

CARNIVALS

The Inhabitants of the District are invited to assist in a

**ROAD CARNIVAL
and
DECORATED PROCESSION**

* *

which will assemble at "Springfield" at the junction of Horndean and New Brighton Roads at 6.30 p.m.

Prizes will be given for the following classes:

Motor Cars	Horses and Traps	Bicycles	Perambulators
Ladies	Gentlemen	Children from 8 to 15 years	

It is proposed to award three prizes in each class where there are more than four entries

The Procession will leave the point of assembly after the judging and parade the Town via North Street, The Square, West Street, and Bath Road to the Marquee in the Sports Ground, where the Prizes will be distributed by Mrs. C. J. JONES.

WATER CARNIVAL

The Mill Pond in West Street will be decorated for the purpose of a Water Carnival, from 9 p.m. to 11 p.m.

Prizes will be awarded for Decorated Boats in two classes:

(i) Fishermen's Boats   (ii) Other Boats

It is proposed to award three Prizes in each class where there are more than four entries.

Intending competitors are requested to notify the Hon. Secretary not later than NOON on SATURDAY, 19th JULY.

**DECORATED PRIVATE HOUSES and
BUSINESS PREMISES**

Three **Prizes** will be given for the Three Best Decorated Private Dwelling Houses and Three **Prizes** for the Best Decorated Business Premises. Judging will commence at 2 p.m. on Saturday, 19 July.

The Committee trust that their fellow townsmen will do their utmost to decorate the Town, and to leave the Flags and Decorations in place until the following Monday evening.

A. J. Horsley, *Chairman, Carnivals Sub-Committee.*
A. E. Madgwick, *Hon. Secretary.*

81 *Peace Celebrations, 1919. The return of peace and the signing of the Treaty of Versailles were marked in Emsworth by these extensive celebrations, which included a road carnival and a water carnival.*

The return of peace led to the lifting of restrictions on fishing. Post-war conditions were however, very difficult for many local businesses. Oyster and scallop fishing resumed. Foster's large sailing vessels such as the *Echo* once again began to sail across to the French coast or along to Beachy Head to dredge for shellfish. The *Evolution*, the *Echo* and the *Nonpareil* continued to operate until the outbreak of the next war in 1939, although another of Foster's vessels, the *Sylvia*, was lost off the French coast with all hands in December 1927 after a collision with a steamer. Kennett also had two fishing ketches operating through the 1920s and 1930s. Foster continued to re-stock his

yster beds; barrels of oyster spat were brought
n from France, Holland and even from America
o be laid down in the harbour. But there were
ewer fishermen in Emsworth after the war and
n 1929 it was said by the Sussex Sea Fisheries
Committee that 'the Emsworth Fisheries have
one backwards'. As the older fishermen died, it
vas no longer an automatic choice for their sons
nd grandsons to follow them into the industry.
even some of those who had become fishermen
vere beginning to find permanent employment
n large yachts. Ernest Boutell, who had been a
isherman since the 1880s, joined the permanent
rew of Lord Fitzwilliam's yacht, *Adela*, in 1926
nd rose to the rank of skipper. Nevertheless,
n the 1930s the remaining fishermen made a
letermined effort to revive their industry. In 1937
0,000 young oysters, obtained from Brittany,
vere laid down in Sweare Deep in an attempt
o re-establish the inshore fishery. In 1939 the
emsworth Dredgermen's Co-operative Society,
vhich had been granted rights over certain
reas of the harbour in the 1871 Fishing Order,
egotiated a deal with the Hayling Island Yacht
Club to allow their craft to be moored over
he oyster beds in return for a fee which was
o be spent on re-stocking. This led to a dispute
vith the local council, which asserted that as
he Harbour Authority it was the only body
vhich could decide on mooring rights within
he harbour, and the question was still unresolved
vhen war began.

Coastal shipping continued its slow, inexorable
lecline. There were occasional visits by colliers
n the 1920s but the last was in 1929. In 1930
n article in the *County Press* lamented that 'the
ig boats have practically left us altogether'. The
maller barges, however, still plied their trade
hrough the port in the 1930s. The working
nills in the town still used water transport for
he carriage of much of the milled flour. In
929 it was said that over 2,000 tons of flour
vere carried away from the Emsworth mills by
arge. When a violent storm caused considerable

82   *Emsworth harbour, early 1920s. Two vessels belonging to Jack Kennett are visible in this photograph. Sailing towards the photographer is the* Tim Whiffler, *a fishing vessel. In the background is the* May, *Kennett's barge, which was used for collecting sand and gravel from the harbour.*

83   *Two of Foster's vessels tied up at Hendy's Quay. On the left is the fishing smack, the* Cymba, *whilst the vessel tied up alongside is his barge, the* Recoil. *The letters J.D.F. are clearly visible on the stern of the* Cymba. *Slipper Mill is just visible on the right of the picture.*

damage in the harbour in September 1935 two
barges, the *Mab* and the *Recoil*, were driven ashore.
Shipbuilding was also a pale shadow of its former
self. Although *Kelly's Directory* of 1931 listed two
shipyards in Emsworth, very few new vessels were
being built. J.D. Foster told an Inquiry in 1929
that his yard had built no new ships since the

84 *Two old fishermen take a rest on the Emsworth foreshore. Taken during the 1920s, this photograph shows the 'winkle penner', used by Foster to store shellfish, in the background.*

85 *The Quay Mill and an Emsworth fishing boat (1935). The mill appears derelict but the fishing boat in the foreground, complete with nets, is still very much in use. (EMHT/Mountfield)*

war. The other yard, by now in the ownership of R. Kemp, seems to have been concentrating on the building and repair of yachts. In 1933, for example, Kemp's yard launched a 90 ft yacht called *Spitfire the Second*. This was in fact a rebuild of an old fishing smack from Scotland.

Apart from oyster and scallop fishing, Foster main business through these years was in timbe Timber was cut and collected from local estate Foster's timber was supplied to customers as fa afield as London, Exeter and Peterborough as we as to a wide range of clients in the local area. I the early 1920s the company found a lucrativ new market for its products in Portsmout Between 1921 and 1923 Foster supplied ove 150,000 wooden paving blocks to the Portsmout Corporation Tramways Department for stree paving. Much sea-seasoned timber was destine for the naval dockyard at Portsmouth to b used as decking for warships. Foster's practic of keeping large logs in the harbour, howeve caused problems for other harbour users. Whe he applied in 1929 for an extension to his leas on the foreshore, many interested local partie voiced their objections at the subsequent Inquir Kemps, the shipbuilders, complained that th floating timber caused damage to their boats. Th same objections were raised by local fisherme and sailing clubs, while the millers told of log which had become wedged into the hatches o the sluices, causing them to cease operations o occasions. During the violent storm in 1935 th floating timber had added to the damage in th harbour by smashing into moored vessels an cutting the mooring ropes of others. Foster application for an extended lease in 1929 wa rejected, but the harbour remained disorganisec The Ark remained as an obstacle to shipping anc apart from some re-booming and the erection c new mooring posts in the early 1920s, little wa done by the council to improve the harbour.

Emsworth's other traditional industries fare little better during the inter-war years. Lumle Mill had been destroyed by fire in 1915. The othe three mills continued working in the 1920s an some modernisation was carried out. The Qua Mill was driven by a gas engine after 1924 bu was forced to cease operations in the 1930s. Th brewery of Kinnell and Hartley also closed in th early 1930s. Rope, sail and sackmaking continue

In 1921 the local council was informed that there were 160 unemployed men in the district, and around Christmas 1934 there were 94 registered unemployed men in Emsworth.

Some unemployment relief schemes were undertaken by the local council; in 1922, for example, new drainage schemes gave employment to a small number of local men. There were also voluntary efforts to help the unemployed. An Emsworth Social Services Council provided a canteen where the unemployed could get meals.

One business that did experience growth in these years was house building. The local council first became involved in the housing issue in 1919 when a Housing Committee was formed. The town still contained a number of houses that were deemed unfit for habitation; one report in 1919 spoke of 28 houses falling into this category. With subsidies available from government the Warblington UDC in 1919 adopted a scheme to build new council houses in the Victoria Road area. About twenty were built and were ready to receive their first tenants in 1922. Nothing was done, however, to remedy the faults of the run-down, overcrowded and insanitary dwellings. Most of these were to be found in Nile Street, South Street, Orange Row and Seaside, although

86 *Albert Prior on the yacht* Dawn Star *(1920s). Like many Emsworth seamen, Albert Prior took employment on the large yachts owned by the rich and famous. The* Dawn Star *was a 70 ft yacht owned by an American banker, Pierrepoint Morgan.*

n the King Street factory. As the traditional ndustries declined few newer trades appeared in he town to provide alternative employment. The own was connected to mains electricity supply rom Portsmouth in 1924 and electrical engineers ppear in the trade directories after this. There vas a growing number of motor engineers within he town, but these new businesses were small cale. The result was that there was a continuing roblem of local unemployment, although not on he scale of the mass unemployment seen in the nore heavily industrialised parts of the country.

87 *Albert Prior, in his yachtsman's uniform, standing on the Emsworth foreshore in the 1920s. The shipyard can be seen in the background.*

88   *Hendy's Quay in the 1920s.*

89   *Foster's log stacks in Bridge Road. Timber that had been brought from local estates was stored in Bridge Road before it was taken to the saw mill. The road surface has been severely damaged by having heavy loads of timber carted along it over many years.*

90   *A cart load of timber in Bridge Road.*

there were also some houses in a very poo state of repair in North Street. The only slur clearance carried out by the local authority wa the demolition of two houses in North Stree in 1935, but the council did undertake a muc larger council house building scheme in th mid-1930s. In 1937 an extensive new housin estate was opened in Victoria Road containin 50 new houses, which could be rented for eigh shillings per week. Meanwhile private housin development continued on the northern an western fringes of Emsworth. One of the large developments was the building of 200 house on the Manor Estate on the northern side c the Havant Road. There was also a new estat the Oaks, which was begun in 1924 with th building of 58 houses.

Despite the poor housing in some parts c the town the health of the district was improving The Medical Officer of Health's report for 192 recorded 33 cases of notifiable diseases during th year, including eight of typhoid. The followin, year there were no recorded cases of death from notifiable diseases, and in 1922 there was not single case of typhoid in the town. Accordin, to the MOH this 'good state of things' was du mainly to 'the improved sanitary arrangements i the district and also to the notices he had issue warning the residents against eating improperl cooked shellfish'. There was also a fall in infan mortality, which the MOH put down to 'the excellent teaching given to mothers at the Infan Welfare Centre', which had been opened by th local authority at the end of the war. Subsequen annual reports by the MOH spoke in glowin, terms of the low death rate and the high lif expectancy of the population of Emsworth and his belief that the town could develop a nev role for itself as a health resort.

The post-war years saw heightened interes in politics in Emsworth. Elections for th Warblington Urban District Council wer more keenly fought than before the war an there was greater involvement of local peopl national politics. This was partly the result of the extension of the franchise in 1918 which gave the right to vote to all adult males and women over the age of 28. The number of electors in the UDC area increased from round 800 to nearer 1,600 and this stimulated the formation of new political groupings and the growing involvement of women. A Women's Co-operative Guild was active throughout the interwar period and a Women's Constitutional (Conservative) Association was formed in 1924. In 1919 the Labour Party made its first appearance in Emsworth and in the council elections in April two Labour candidates headed the poll. The *County Press* commented on the 'energetic manner in which they set about securing their election'. One of the new councillors, William Bartlett, immediately made an impact on the council by pushing strongly for the building of council houses. In the following year the Labour party put up four candidates for election to the council, but the emergence of this new political force disturbed the comfortable complacency of the business interests who had dominated local politics before the war. A branch of the Middle Classes Union was established to 'attack the forces of socialism', and all four Labour candidates were defeated in 1921 in a record turnout for Warblington UDC election. Four out of the five MCU candidates were elected. Many of the leading figures in this Middle Classes Union, such as Dr Lockhart Stephens, were in fact Conservatives, but they fought under a different banner in local politics. The MCU (renamed the National Citizens Union in 1922) continued to enjoy success for the next two years, but by 1924 poor attendance and apathy had led to the disbanding of the organisation.

The mid-1920s were quiet years in local politics, there being no contests in 1924 or 1925. By 1928, however, local elections were again being contested vigorously. In that year there were no fewer than 13 candidates for six vacant seats, and this contest saw the election of

91 *Some of Foster's vessels tied up in the Slipper. The barge* Recoil *is on the left. In the background is the 'Big Bunny' millpond in which Foster stored timber for sea seasoning.*

92 *The Quay Mill. The chimney on the left shows that the mill's owners have installed an auxiliary source of power to keep the mill working when water power is not available.*

the first (and only) woman councillor on the Warblington UDC. Miss Onslow, a cousin of Sir Thomas Inskip, who for many years had been the M.P. for the area, was already well known in local circles for her work as a school manager and her energetic work on behalf of the Victoria Cottage Hospital. The late 1920s also saw the emergence of a renewed Ratepayers' Association which made all the running in local politics in the next few years. Committed to keeping the rates as low as possible, the Ratepayers' Association

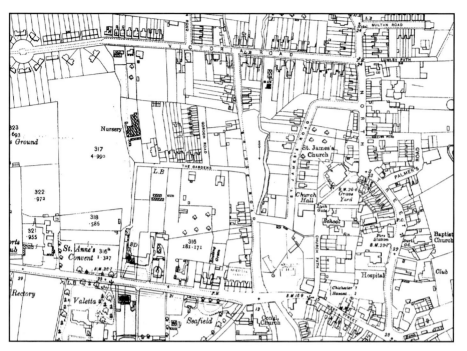

93 *Part of the 1932 O.S. map. Since the 1910 map was published there has been considerable development in the north-western corner of the town. Victoria Road has been extended and many new houses built. There has also been development in Washington Road, Bridge Road, Gordon Road and the Gardens. A new school has been built in Washington Road. (Hampshire Record Office)*

secured the election of three of its candidates in 1929 and four in 1930. Councillors who were also members of the Ratepayers' Association were expected to vote in accordance with its wishes, and the meetings of the Association became the main forum for political debate in the town. One effect of the growing domination of local politics by organised groups, however, was that genuine Independents, such as Jack Kennett, who had served the town for many years, were squeezed out. Kennett lost his seat on the council in 1921. He regained a seat in 1926, only to be defeated again in 1929 when the Ratepayers' Association dominated the poll.

In 1932 local government in the area was reorganised. The Warblington UDC was swept away and a new Havant and Waterloo UDC was formed to administer a large area of south-east Hampshire. Emsworth was represented on the new body by three councillors. The effect of removing control over local affairs from Emsworth to Havant was gradually to erode interest in the local political process. By the mid-1930s local elections were again uncontested and in 1939 attendance at

94 *An art deco façade in central Emsworth. This building on the corner of North Street and West Street is a rare local example of the art deco style, popular in the inter-war years.*

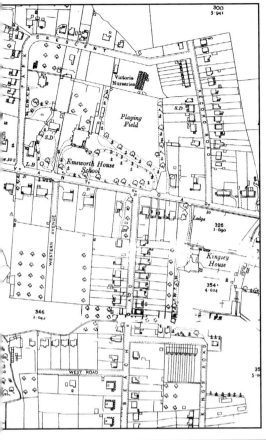

Ratepayers' Association meetings had fallen to such an extent that there were fears it would be forced to disband. The change also worked to the disadvantage of women. Miss Onslow, who had been re-elected to the Warblington UDC in 1931, did not secure a seat on the new body and there were no other women councillors during its early years.

The incorporation of Emsworth into a much larger unit of local government, after less than forty years of local self-government, was one of a number of changes that affected the character of the town at this time. In 1928 the parishes of Emsworth and Warblington were merged again but, in recognition of the historical importance of Warblington, the new parish was called Warblington-with-Emsworth. We have already seen how many of the traditional industries of the town were struggling to survive in the inter-war years. The shopkeepers of the town were also experiencing growing difficulty in competing with the larger stores that were available in Portsmouth. Regular bus services to Portsmouth operated by Southdown Motor

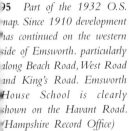

95   *Part of the 1932 O.S. map. Since 1910 development has continued on the western side of Emsworth. particularly along Beach Road, West Road and King's Road. Emsworth House School is clearly shown on the Havant Road. (Hampshire Record Office)*

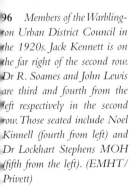

96   *Members of the Warblington Urban District Council in the 1920s. Jack Kennett is on the far right of the second row. Dr R. Soames and John Lewis are third and fourth from the left respectively in the second row. Those seated include Noel Kinnell (fourth from left) and Dr Lockhart Stephens MOH (fifth from the left). (EMHT/ Privett)*

HANTS & SUSSEX

MOTOR SERVICES LIMITED

Super Luxury Radio

COACHES

For Outings, Dances and All Events

SPECIAL RATES FOR PARTIES

Any Number :: Any Time :: Any Distance

Comfort — Reliability — Safety

Apply—HEAD OFFICE, B. S. WILLIAMS, Managing Director
South Leigh Road, Emsworth.   Telephone 415

Depot : Sultan Road, Emsworth

97 *An advert for Hants and Sussex Motor Services, 1930s. This local bus company was established by Basil Williams and Arthur Pennicutt in 1937 to provide services that the much larger Southdown bus company did not offer.*

Services had begun in 1916; the train service through Emsworth had been increased in 1901 and was further improved in the 1930s with the electrification of the railway line. Improvements in transport meant that local residents could work, shop and be entertained in Portsmouth more easily. Local businesses, however, took up the challenge. A local Shopping Week was organised by traders in 1928 and repeated in following years. The Town Hall began to be used as a cinema in 1918 and continued to offer local cinema-goers an alternative to the larger venues in Portsmouth throughout the inter-war years. In

1930 the Pavilion Cinema, as it was now called, was completely overhauled with the addition of a balcony and plush seats and the installation of sound equipment for the new 'talkies'. When the millpond was no longer required by Dittman and Malpass for the running of their machinery at the Quay Mill, it was offered to the local council in 1924 to purchase as a public amenity. With a gift of £500 from Noel Kinnell, of Kinnell and Hartley brewery, the town was able to purchase the millpond and carry out improvements to the sea-wall. In subsequent years the millpond became a popular and attractive local amenity with boats for hire, although the vision of the *County Press* for an Emsworth Aquatic Park, with a water chute, swimming and diving as well as boating, never came to fruition.

The early post-war years saw the creation of two sailing clubs in Emsworth, events which were to have some significance for the future development of the town. In 1919 the Emsworth Sailing Club was founded by a group of retired military officers, many of whom had served in the Brigade of Guards in the Great War. Membership, which was limited to 500, was offered to members of gentlemen's clubs. Of the 74 enrolled members

98 *Basil Williams, the co-founder of the Hants and Sussex bus company. He applied for his first licence to operate a bus service, when still only twenty, in 1934. It was not until 1938 that the company was successful in gaining a licence to run a service between Emsworth and Thorney Island.*

99 *George Gale, founder of the Pavilion Cinema. Mr Gale, a sailmaker working for John Lewis, ran the cinema when it first started showing lantern slides and, later, in the silent film era. (EMHT/Downing)*

who had joined by 1923, 38 were local people, 17 came from London and nine were described as 'county' members. The rather exclusive nature of the early membership was underlined by the relatively high entrance fees: life membership cost £25 whilst 'ordinary' members had to pay a two-guinea entrance fee and one guinea per annum. The new Sailing Club was a success. The bathing house at the end of Bath Road was bought and converted for use as a clubhouse, and regular sailing races and the annual regatta became an established part of the summer social scene in Emsworth. By 1932 the Emsworth Sailing Club had more than 200 members. As well as the regattas organised by the club itself, the facilities were also used each summer by sailing enthusiasts from the Household Cavalry for their own regattas.

There had been attempts by sailing enthusiasts in Emsworth to form a sailing club since at least the 1890s. Most of those involved had been local businessmen, but also included were some of the fishermen. In 1912 an Emsworth Sailing Committee was formed to organise races but these activities had to be suspended when war broke out in 1914. Racing resumed in 1919, and in 1921 the Emsworth Mud Slippers Sailing Club was founded at a meeting in the *Ship Inn*. With an

100 *An advertisement for the Pavilion Cinema, 1932. The cinema was converted to show 'talkies' in 1930 and continued to provide entertainment for the people of the area until the early 1950s.*

101 *Noel Kinnell's gift to the town. This plaque commemorates the generosity of Noel Kinnell, who, after selling the Seaside Millpond to the W.U.D.C. in 1925, agreed to cover the cost of rebuilding the sea wall and the promenade. (EMHT/Privett)*

EMSWORTH
SLIPPER SAILING CLUB

Head Quarters,
The Ship Inn,
March, 1925.

Dear Sir or Madam,

    I have pleasure in sending you a copy of the Balance Sheet for 1924.

    The Committee would be glad if you will support the Club, and any donation or subscription will be gratefully received by the Hon. Secretary, or may be paid direct to the Hon. Treasurer, at Lloyds Bank Limited, Emsworth.

    Yours faithfully,
        B. F. JONES,
          Hon. Secretary.

102   *The Seaside Millpond. The millpond is one of the town's most picturesque features today and helps to give Emsworth its special character. The large building jutting out into the pond in the distance is an old malthouse, which is now used by the Emsworth Slipper Sailing Club for storing boats.*

103   *Emsworth Slipper Sailing Club. The club was established as the Emsworth Mud Slippers Sailing Club in 1921, using the* Ship Inn *as its headquarters in the absence of its own clubhouse. After experiencing difficulties in sustaining the club in the 1920s, the ESSC was placed on a more permanent footing in 1933.*

annual subscription of five shillings, membership was theoretically within the reach of a broader spectrum of local society than the Emsworth Sailing Club, but by 1923 there were only 29 members. With limited funds and no permanent base, the early years of the Mud Slippers proved difficult and the club's activities were suspended in 1925. It was not until 1933 that the renamed Emsworth Slipper Sailing and Motor Boat Club was reformed and twice-weekly racing began again. Regattas then became annual events, and

104 *Emsworth High Street in the 1920s. This is the view looking east towards* the Black Dog Inn, *with the colonnaded porch of the* Crown Hotel *on the left. Note the absence of traffic.*

from 1935 included swimming and rowing races for children. By September 1939, when sailing was suspended for the duration of the war, both the Emsworth Sailing Club and the Slipper Sailing Club had become firmly established.

The inter-war years saw the decline of many of Emsworth's traditional trades. By 1939 the big boats no longer called at the town's quays. Fewer of the town's residents depended on the sea for their livelihoods by 1939 than had been the case in 1914, whilst a much higher proportion of the population lived in Emsworth but worked elsewhere. Much of the town had indeed developed into a 'residential suburb', as had been predicted in 1891, but the heart of the town, around the High Street, South Street, and King Street still retained much of its traditional character.

105 *The Square in the 1920s. Among the group in the centre is Birky Miller, a well known local character, with his pet heron and chicken. The local press reported that every July Birky Miller and his pets entertained the charabanc parties on their way home from Goodwood Races.*

WARBLINGTON-WITH-EMSWORTH PARISH MAGAZINE.

PINK'S TEAS are the nicest.

Save Pink's Coupons and Save Money.

Local Branch: 23. HIGH STREET, EMSWORTH.
Telephone, EMSWORTH 18.

PINKS' GUARANTEE : Any Goods which do not give complete satisfaction may be returned, and
others will be given in exchange, or the money paid returned in full provided the goods are returned.

Dittman & Malpas, Ltd.
Queen Street & Quay Mills, Emsworth.
West Street & Havant Mills, Havant.

Corn, Forage and Seed
Merchants.

Telephone 95 Emsworth.
„   47 Havant.   Garden Seeds a Speciality

Established Quarter Century.

AMOR'S Stores
HIGH ST., EMSWORTH,
For QUALITY in
GROCERIES, PROVISIONS, FRUIT
AND VEGETABLES.

Phone 112   Agent for Fullers' High-Class Cakes.

———Telephone 118———

SCADGELL & SON,
FUNERAL DIRECTORS.
Complete House Furnishers.
Cabinet Makers and Upholsterers.
Decorators and Plumbers - -
Builders and Painters.
The Square,   EMSWORTH.

G. DAVIS & SONS
Bakers.
38, QUEEN St. & 26, HIGH St., EMSWORTH,
For BREAD you will really enjoy !
Send us a Postcard—and we'll be pleased to call.

G. E. MILLER,
Builder and Decorator,
"KARVILLE," KING'S ROAD, EMSWORTH.
HOUSE REPAIRS.
Personal Attention.   Charges Moderate.

James Critchett,
Victoria Road, Emsworth.
UNDERTAKER. UPHOLSTERER.

General Repairs to House Property.
Painting and General House Decorating.

Telephone 58.

A. M. NEWELL
Family Butcher,

1, High St., Emsworth

YOU CAN'T BEAT THE

BRUNSWICK
CLEANERS
For SPEED, QUALITY & PRICE.
55, HIGH STREET, EMSWORTH.

W. VOYSEY,
SPECIALISING in FOOTWEAR of QUALITY.
———Efficient Repair Service———
48, High Street, EMSWORTH

EAT MORE FISH.
For First-Class Quality
FISH AND CHIPS
TRY **NORTH STREET FISHERIES.**
OPEN AT 7 O'CLOCK
Cleanliness and Purity Guaranteed.

106   *Advertisements for local stores, 1932. This page from
the parish magazine illustrates the traditional range of shops
that were available in the High Street and St Peter's Square.
(Portsmouth City Record Office)*

107   *Emsworth High Street, 1930s. Corbin's Shoe and
Clothing Stores, on the right, was a long established Emsworth
business. Scadgell and Sons is on the left of the picture
behind the parked vehicle.*

EMSWORTH'S
GALA DAY
To celebrate
HIS MAJESTY'S SILVER JUBILEE
ON MONDAY NEXT
ON THE
Recreation Ground
Under the patronage of Sir Harold & Lady Pink

:···:
GREAT ATTRACTIONS
:···:

Lunch at 12.30 for the Old Folk
Tea for the Young Folks at 4 p.m.

**Sports Competitions and Sideshows for
ALL from 2 to 8 p.m.   Over 70 prizes**

CONCERT FOR OLD FOLKS at 7.30 p,m.
OPEN AIR DANCING 9 to 10.30 p.m.
FIREWORKS DISPLAY at 10.30 p.m.

:: **ADMISSION FREE TO ALL** ::

Refreshments at Moderate Prices may be obtained on the Ground

108 *(above)   Floods in the 1930s. High spring tides often brought flooding to the Mud Island and Slipper areas on either side of the millpond. This picture, taken from a vantage point at the bottom of Queen Street, shows lorries cautiously trying to cross the bridge, watched by a crowd of interested spectators.*

109 *(left)   The Silver Jubilee Gala Day, 1935. Emsworth celebrated in traditional style.*

110 *(below)   Coronation celebrations, 1937. The coronation of George VI was celebrated by Emsworthians with their usual gusto. This children's fancy dress parade is passing along Record Road. (EMHT/Downing)*

1939 EMPIRE AIR DAY 1939

ROYAL AIR FORCE, THORNEY ISLAND

Price 2d.   LOCAL PROGRAMME   Price 2d.

The Royal Air Force first occupied this Station at Thorney Island in February, 1938. In May of the same year is was officially visited by His Majesty the King. This year, for the first time, it is being thrown open to the public.

Apart from the flying programme that has been arranged, certain buildings are also open for inspection; these include:—

A BARRACK ROOM (i.e. a living and sleeping room)
THE DINING HALL.
THE INSTITUTE REFRESHMENT BAR.
THE INSTITUTE BILLIARD ROOM.
THE INSTITUTE LIBRARY & READING ROOM.
THE TORPEDO SECTION.

111 *Empire Air Day, 1939. The RAF station at Thorney Island was opened in 1938. Local people had their first chance to look around the base in the summer of 1939 on Empire Air Day. The reference to the 'Torpedo Section' indicates that Thorney Island was a Coastal Command base preparing for anti-submarine operations.*

112 *The inauguration of the bus service to Thorney Island, February 1939. After years of frustration, the Hants and Sussex bus company was granted a licence to run a scheduled service to Thorney Island and the service began on 27 February 1939. This photograph shows Sqn Ldr Dewar cutting the tape at the Thorney Island end of the route.*

IX

1939 to the Present Day

Change and Continuity

Even before the outbreak of war in September 1939 plans for air-raid precautions had been made. In June the council began to identify sites for large communal shelters – one was to be built near the Baptist Church in North Street and another in the King Street area – and ARP warden posts had been established in four parts of the town.

When war actually began, however, many of the planned shelters had not yet been completed. The Council School was unable to open for the autumn term until 25 September because the air-raid shelters had not been finished. When the school did reopen it was faced with an immediate influx of children who had been evacuated from

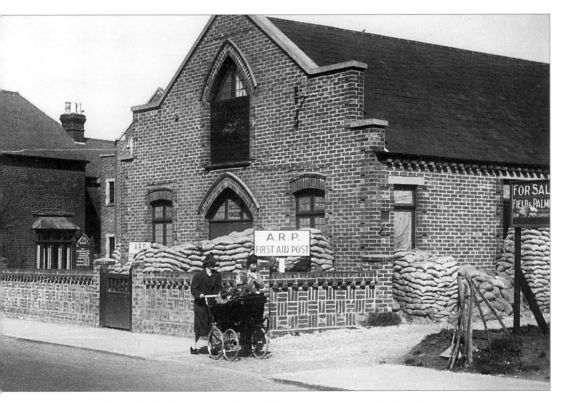

113   *An ARP post at the Baptist Church in North Street. (EMHT/Soames)*

114 *A young schoolgirl carries her gas mask with her to school. This photograph shows Christine Gale at Washington Road School. (EMHT/Downing)*

areas considered to be at high risk of air raids and who were staying with relatives or family friends in Emsworth. Thirty-two were admitted on the first day of term alone and a further 17 arrived during the next three days. The blackout regulations were vigorously enforced by the local police and there was a number of prosecutions

for breaches of the regulations in the first few weeks of the war. Conscription was already in place before war began and there was a steady stream of young men from Emsworth called up for service in the forces. Requisitioning also made an impact, Emsworth House School having to be closed when the Admiralty took over the building for use as a research facility.

Emsworth was not a major centre of population and had few industries and so was not itself a primary target for German bombers. On the other hand, being situated on the south coast near to a large RAF base at Thorney Island and a major Royal Navy base and dockyard at Portsmouth, it was uncomfortably close to some of the fiercest aerial battles of the early stages of the war. In the summer of 1940, after the fall of France and with the threat of invasion looming, the head teacher of the Council School was instructed by the police to stop using the school bell; henceforth the ringing of bells would be a warning that the invasion had begun. But it was air-raid sirens that most disturbed the peace of the town during that summer. Since the press were prohibited from reporting details of air raids the best source of evidence about what was actually happening in Emsworth during the Battle of Britain and the Blitz which followed is the log book kept by the head teacher of the Council School. His first reference to an air-raid warning was on 20 June 1940. He reported that there had been an alert the previous night lasting from 11.30 p.m. until 3.30 a.m., as a consequence of which attendance at school on that day was very low. For the next month, until the end of term, the log book records air-raid warnings on a daily basis, some during the night and others during the school day. On 3 July, for example, the siren sounded 'just as we started prayers'. On 12 July the warning sounded at around 6 p.m. and there was 'anti-aircraft and machine gun fire almost immediately. Many bullets and shell fragments were picked up.' On 22 July, at 9.20 p.m., 'enemy planes travelling east and south of us were heavily

115 *A Hawker Hector aircraft at Thorney Island. This photograph was taken soon after the station opened in 1938. (Imperial War Museum Ref. HU 8592)*

116 *An aerial view of the new RAF station on Thorney Island, also taken in 1938. The construction of the base provided employment for many local people. (Imperial War Museum, Ref. HU 8605)*

117 *RAF personnel catch the bus from Emsworth. This wartime picture of buses waiting in Sultan Road shows how busy the service became during wartime. Although there was a half-hourly service between Emsworth station and the base, at times it was necessary to use relief buses to cope with the sheer numbers of personnel passing through on their way to Thorney Island.*

fired on by anti-aircraft defences. Heavy explosions were heard but no warning was sounded.'

The Council School closed for the summer holidays on 26 July and for August, when the Battle of Britain was reaching its climax, the Log was not being kept. However, other evidence gives an insight into the intensity of the battle which was fought in the skies around Emsworth at that time. The diary of Strachan Soames records that between 15 August and 21 September the air-raid siren sounded 86 times. On 16 August alone there were six air-raid warnings. The nearby RAF station on Thorney Island was first attacked on 13 August when a lone German raider dropped bombs on the airfield. Opened in 1938, Thorney Island was mainly used as a base for Coastal Command aircraft engaged in anti-submarine patrols in the Channel but, in June 1940, the station also became a base for Blenheim fighter-bombers which were used for bombing attacks against French ports and air-

defence duties. The biggest attack on the airfiel was on Sunday 18 August when 28 Stuka dive bombers, escorted by Me 109 fighters, cause serious damage, destroying two hangars, sever aircraft and a fuel dump. The station was attacke again on 23 August by Junker 88 bombers.

The Battle of Britain continued unt the middle of September, but even after th danger of invasion had receded the threat c air raids was a constant factor in the lives of th townspeople. During the autumn and winter c 1940-1 Portsmouth suffered several air raids, an the bombing was particularly severe in Januar 1941. The noise of the bombs exploding and th anti-aircraft fire could be heard from Emswortl whilst the fires from burning buildings could b clearly seen in the night skies. WVS members fror Emsworth were called upon to give assistance i Portsmouth whilst the Council School receive warnings to stand by for evacuees. All throug this period, however, no bombs actually fell o

118 *Beaufort aircraft of No. 22 Squadron being prepared for a patrol. This squadron was based at Thorney Island during 1941 and flew anti-submarine patrols. (Imperial War Museum, HU 3647)*

Emsworth itself. That changed on the night of 7 April 1941, when a German bomber dropped a number of incendiary and high explosive bombs on and near the town. The School Log reported that 'Practically all of the shop fronts were blown out and in South Street, Tower Street and King Street many of the roofs were severely damaged.' During this raid the house of Jack Kennett by the harbour was one of those which were severely damaged and several fishing boats in the harbour were destroyed. The Council School was used to accommodate overnight those whose houses had been damaged.

The danger of air attacks continued until the summer of 1944. Emsworth suffered three further strikes by German planes in 1943 and 1944. In February 1943 the School Log recorded the sighting of a German plane coming 'from the direction of Havant, flying very low and just the other side of the railway and apparently machine gunning. At 4.38 p.m. another came on about the same course and appeared to machine gun the houses in Horndean Road.' A more serious raid took place in August 1943. 'About 1 a.m. bombs were dropped in the town and several houses were more or less destroyed. The school was prepared for the homeless and over thirty people slept here.' This was the raid when the Bath Road area was hit and an unexploded bomb had to be dealt with in the aftermath. The final raid to hit Emsworth itself was in February 1944, when the School Log recorded that one of the pupils had been 'badly hurt by a piece of bomb during the raid last night. His house was damaged and the bungalow next to it was practically destroyed.' This was the only injury actually recorded in the raids on Emsworth, although there would undoubtedly have been more. Most of the air-raid warnings were sounded when enemy planes were passing overhead on their way to centres of population to the north and west, and the greatest impact on most people was the disruption to their lives and the fear of being attacked. In the summer of 1944 a new danger appeared, the flying bombs, several of which were seen passing over, or near to, Emsworth. The first recorded sighting was on 25 June in the evening, followed by another on 3 July in the middle of the day. On 11 July the School Log recorded the sighting of 11 flying bombs during the day, but none actually fell on Emsworth. By the end of the month, with Allied forces advancing through France and capturing the launch sites, the danger from flying bombs was receding, and the last months of the war were free of air-raid warnings.

Inevitably the war caused disruption to the economic life of the town. Foster's fishing smacks were again laid up for the duration of the war. J.D. Foster died in May 1940, and the large and successful oyster fishing business which he had established 60 years before was finally laid to rest. Other parts of his business, however, such as the supply of timber, continued under new management. Those fishermen who were too old for active service continued to fish within the harbour. In September 1940 one such fisherman, Harry Treagust, rescued an RAF pilot from the water after his aircraft had been shot down. Another fisherman, Harry Parham, was taken on by the Admiralty to direct naval personnel in cable-laying operations in the harbour. The laying of cables and large concrete blocks on the sea bed, as obstacles to submarines and invasion barges, presented the fishermen with yet more difficulties in the way of their normal dredging operations, however. The fishing industry's decline was hastened by the war. Some local industries, on the other hand, were presented with new opportunities. The shipyard was engaged in building small naval assault craft, whilst the firm of Searle Sub-Assembly (Aircraft) set up a new factory in West Road making components for the aircraft industry. This was a satellite factory built in Emsworth by a London-based company which gave employment to 40 people. It produced

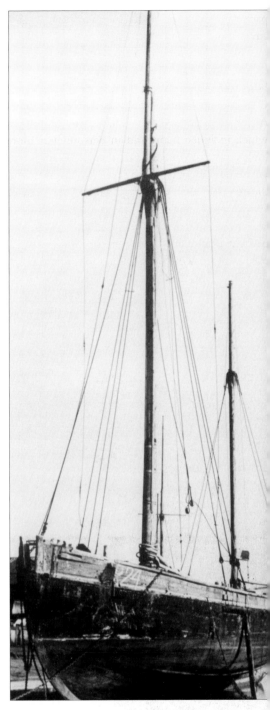

119 *The* Nonpareil. *Foster's fishing fleet was taken out of service when war broke out. This photograph shows the* Nonpareil *laid up in the autumn of 1939. (EMHT/ Mountfield)*

parts for Stirling bombers, fuel tanks for training aircraft and ammunition boxes.

The war brought many Allied servicemen to the Emsworth area. RAF Thorney Island was host, at various times, to squadrons of the Royal Canadian Air force, the Royal New Zealand Airforce and to the Mysore Squadron of Spitfires, which included many Indian personnel. A more long-term presence was the French Navy's camp, which was established in 1942 to the north of the town in the Southleigh Road area. Named Bir Hacheim, the camp was home to hundreds of French sailors for the next four years. The participation of these sailors in sporting and social events in Emsworth underlined the international dimension of the Allied war effort. During a 'Wings for Victory' fund-raising week in May 1943, Free French sailors joined in the sports competitions and a rendition of the Marseillaise by a sailor at the opening parade was enthusiastically applauded. A year later a parade to launch the 'Salute the Soldier' week included a detachment of Free French sailors. The French sailors entered a football team in local tournaments. Tony Wilson, who lived in Horndean Road, was described as the manager of the Free French Navy's Sports Section. A former featherweight boxing champion himself, he successfully promoted Anglo-French boxing tournaments in the area and managed a highly successful French Navy boxing team.

The end of the war in Europe on 8 May 1945 saw Emsworth, in common with every other town and village in the country, given over to celebrations. The schools and businesses were closed for two days and by nightfall on VE Day 'the town was festooned with flags and bunting from end to end'. The *County Press* reporter noted that during the day the atmosphere in the town was rather subdued, but 'as the evening wore on people began to let themselves go and the streets

120   *French sailors enjoying a game of cards in one of the barrack blocks at the Free French Naval Camp.*

121 *Inauguration of the new War Memorial, 1950. After the First World War, Emsworth's war memorial was a plaque installed in St James's Church. In December 1950 this shelter, designed by Peter Elcock (second from left), was built in St Peter's Square to commemorate Emsworth's war dead. The group includes the Chairman of HWUDC (third from left) and members of the British Legion, including Mrs Meredith (far right) and Miss Stott (fourth from right).*

122 *A Remembrance Day parade in the 1950s. This part of the parade is led by the nurses from the Cottage Hospital. The Women's Police Force is in the background.*

123 *Beacon Square in the 1950s. Beacon Square, one of the post-war housing developments in Emsworth, is shown here soon after the estate was built. (Hampshire Record Office, Ref. 43M94/42/55)*

were lively with parties singing and dancing'. On 9 May there was a fireworks display on the quay in the evening, and at the weekend the street parties began. King Street was the first area to organise its party – the *County Press* reported that the street 'went berzerk' – whilst in other parts of the town street parties were still being held in the middle of June. Scarcely had the town had time to complete all the VE celebrations than VJ Day was announced in the middle of August. This time the *County Press* described the celebrations as 'hearty and spontaneous': in traditional Emsworth fashion parties of youths paraded around the town banging drums and other instruments, there was a large bonfire in the Square, and 'any amount of fireworks'. Street parties, some of which were still being held in September, completed the celebrations of the return of peace.

Gradually the pattern of life in post-war Emsworth began to recover some semblance of normality. One of the most urgent priorities for local government, even in an area which had sustained very little bomb damage, was to address the serious shortage of housing. One short-term method of relieving the housing shortage was to convert former military camps into civilian housing. Southleigh Camp was released by the Admiralty in June 1945 and there were plans to convert the huts into civilian dwellings. Before the work had begun, however, in August 1946 several homeless families from the area moved into the camp as squatters. This prompted the Admiralty to place an armed guard on a similar camp at West Leigh near Havant. The Free French camp was vacated by French sailors in 1946, but was then occupied by Polish ex-servicemen until 1951. Work on building council houses had begun by 1947 and a number of new estates took shape, including one in the Gardens area and much larger estates in the area of New Brighton and Southleigh Roads. In August 1953 the HWUDC

124   *Sailing dinghies at the Town Quay, 1960s.*

125   *An Emsworth Slipper Sailing Club bulletin from 1978, showing the former* Anchor Inn *as the club's headquarters.*

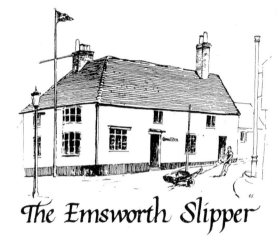

The Emsworth Slipper

EMSWORTH SLIPPER SAILING CLUB, THE ANCHOR, SOUTH STREET, EMSWORTH

VOLUME 2.   No. 2.   APRIL 1978

Commodore: Peter Hamey   Vice Commodore: Lionel Payne
Rear Commodore Sailing: Jim Holt.
Rear Commodore Admin.   Michael Hackman
Secretary: Marilyn Hackman   Treasurer: Roslyn Speed-Andrews
Social Secretary: David and Trisha Divers   Bosun: Stan Buck
Chairman & Sailing Secretary: Andrew Turner

Editor: Neil Baxter
-------oOo-------

Committee

Neil Baxter   Derek Cooper
Peter Gatfield   George Ient
Sid Jelley   Roger Plumb
Ian Porter   Chris Tarrant
Colin Urry   David Urry
-------oOo-------

completed its one thousandth post-war council house in Hollybank Lane, on the site of the former Free French naval camp. Despite the progress in house building, however, there were still 1,634 families on the housing waiting list in November 1953.

Pleasure sailing resumed in the summer of 1945 and the Emsworth Sailing Club was able to hold its first post-war races in August, although at first with only a handful of competitors. The Emsworth Slipper Sailing Club was not able to resume its activities until the summer of 1946. Restrictions on fishing were lifted, although not all of the fishermen were able to return to their pre-war trade. Ernest Parham, for example, was forced to give up fishing since his boat had been destroyed in an air raid, although one of the oldest fishermen, Harry Prior, had just

126 *A sailing regatta in the 1950s. This race, for Firefly boats, was one of the fixtures in the ESSC regatta.*

127 *A wintry scene at the* Anchor, *1978. In the late 1970s the ESSC was in the process of purchasing the Quay Mill as its new headquarters and the* Anchor *was put up for sale.*

completed building a new boat when he passed on in 1946. Dredging for oysters in the harbour now faced the extra difficulties posed by large concrete blocks laid on the sea bed during the war, which were still causing problems in the early 1950s. Indeed harbour users, including both fishermen and pleasure sailors, were becoming increasingly frustrated with the poor state of the harbour after years of neglect. In September 1945 the Emsworth Sailing Club complained to the council about the many broken mooring posts, the stumps of which were a serious hazard for sailors. In 1947 the Emsworth Slipper Sailing Club complained about the poor state of the booms in the harbour, whilst the fishermen made more attempts to persuade the authorities to remove the sunken concrete blocks. In 1947 the Hayling Island Sailing Club revived its pre-war plan for moorings for yachts in Mill Rythe, where the oyster fishermen had long held fishing rights. The fishermen, through the Emsworth Dredgermen's Co-operative Society, again launched a staunch defence of their interests: 'We want to work in harmony with the yachtsmen,' said the fishermen's spokesman, 'but we must safeguard the livelihood of our fishermen.' When the issue was finally settled by the Ministry of Transport the mooring posts for the yachts were sited away from the main oyster beds and the interests of both parties were protected. The poor state of the harbour and continuing disputes between harbour users finally prompted the HWUDC in 1953 to set up a Harbour Improvement Committee. A Harbour Master was appointed more than fifty years after the last one had resigned and repairs were made to the mooring posts and booms. In 1966 the council purchased or leased many acres of mud flats within the harbour in order to extend its control.

The war had severely damaged the local fishing industry. In 1939 Jack Kennett had lost 90,000 oysters in his beds near Hayling Island because wartime restrictions prevented their recovery. J.D. Foster died in 1940 and Jack Kennett

128 *The Boutell brothers. Both of these men had worked on Foster's fishing smacks, and their father had been captain of both the* Evolution *and the* Cymba.

in 1945, and their oyster smacks did not resume fishing when peace returned. Through the post-war years other local fishermen made a number of attempts to revive the fortunes of their industry. In 1957 efforts were made, with help from the Ministry of Fisheries, to clean the oyster beds by dredging and in the following year seed oysters were purchased to restock the grounds. A further attempt was made in 1970 when the Emsworth Harbour Fishermen's Federation bought 20,000

129 The Nonpareil, 1950. Foster's fleet of fishing smacks did not return to sea after the end of the Second World War and all were abandoned to decay on the Emsworth mud. (EMHT/ Mountfield)

130 *The Emsworth Marina. Shown here soon after it was opened in 1964 in Foster's former log pond, the marina attracted even greater numbers of recreational sailors to Emsworth in the summer months, and stimulated the building of new waterside housing developments.*

seed oysters for laying down in Sweare Deep. Efforts to revive the industry were accompanied by a determination to protect the interests of the fishermen from encroachments by other harbour users. The dispute with the Hayling Island Sailing Club broke out again in 1957. In 1961 the fishermen voiced strong objections to the plan to build a new marina in Emsworth, arguing that the many additional boats which would use the harbour would pose a threat to the oyster beds through oil and sewage discharges. By the 1960s, however, the fishermen were no longer the force they had once been and, despite their objections, the marina was built. Even so, in 1984 local fishermen landed over 33 tons of oysters at Emsworth, valued at over £56,000.

The tradition of boat building in Emsworth has continued through the post-war years. In the 1950s the two main Emsworth boat-building firms were J.G. Parham, based at Dolphin Quay, and Aero-Marine in King Street. Both concentrated on the building of wooden sailing craft and both gained an international reputation. In 1956 Parhams supplied an all-teak sailing sloop for a customer in the Bahamas. Aero-Marine exhibited their craft at the Earls Court Boat Show in the 1950s. In 1957 their exhibits included a five-ton ocean racer and a 19 ft fast cruiser. Under the ownership of Rear-Admiral Gick, another Emsworth boatyard was one of the pioneers in the use of concrete in boat construction. In 1970 the yard completed an 18 ft survey launch using a new technique which involved spraying a mixture of cement powder and chopped glass fibre onto a mould.

In general, however, industry in Emsworth has continued its decline since the post-war years. Planning applications by a number of industrial concerns were being rejected by the council after 1945. The wartime Searle Aircraft factory in West Road was forced to close after the council refused permission for permanent industrial use.

131   *Dolphin Quay, 1950s. This postcard view shows the boat-building and repair yard of J.G. Parham, with traditional wooden-hulled sailing yachts moored alongside. (Hampshire Record Office 43M94/42/27)*

132 *Emsworth fishermen, December 1961. Charles Treagust and Jack Savage display their oyster catch on the Town Quay, keeping alive a long tradition among fishermen in Emsworth.*

134 *Dolphin Quay today. Now under new ownership, the boat repair yard at Dolphin Quay is still a flourishing business.*

J. G. PARHAM & SONS

Queen Street — EMSWORTH — Hants

High-class Boat Builders

Repairs and Conversions a speciality— 40 years' experience

133 *Advertisement for J.G. Parham, boat builders, from the 1950s.*

135 *Emsworth Square in the 1950s. The War Memorial shelter has pride of place at the top of the picture, but the centre of the Square has been turned into a car park, detracting from the overall attractiveness of this traditional town centre. (Hampshire Record Office, Ref. 43M94/42/45)*

136 *In 1949 the Hants and Sussex bus company began a new Emsworth town bus service to connect the Victoria Road estate with the Square. The company had prospered during the war from government contracts and the post-war years saw further rapid expansion. Through a series of acquisitions of other bus and coach operators, Basil Williams built up a fleet of over 150 vehicles, serving an extensive area in Hampshire and West Sussex.*

137 *Emsworth High Street, c.1949. In this scene buses belonging to the Emsworth-based Hants and Sussex bus company are operating local services through the centre of the town.*

An application by a firm to install power tools such as circular saws at Dolphin Quay, and another in 1950 to use a workshop in Sultan Road for furniture making, were rejected after objections from local residents about the potential noise from the sites. Emsworth's development as a mainly residential area was being reinforced and underlined by these planning controls.

In the 1950s a proposal to build a short bypass road on the main A27 south coast trunk road through Emsworth became a major issue for the town. The congestion on this road and the dangers to road users had been a serious concern even before the war. In 1922 the WUDC had applied for permission to impose a 10mph speed limit through Emsworth because of 'the dangerous speed at which some motor drivers approach the town and pass through it'. This request had been refused and, apart from some road straightening and widening at the *Black*

Dog corner in the Square, little was done to improve the road in the inter-war period. In the 1930s the stretch of road which caused the most concern was that between Emsworth and Havant where, due to the increase in traffic, accidents had become so frequent that the *County Press* began to refer to it as 'the death-trap road'. During the 1950s and 1960s the steady increase in road traffic meant that Emsworth became, especially at peak periods, a notorious bottleneck on the main south coast road. Hampshire County Council had begun considering a proposal for a 'short by-pass' through Emsworth slightly to the north of the existing road in 1934, and this idea was revived in 1952. But the idea was strongly opposed by many Emsworth people on the grounds that it would split the community: 'The proposed road is not a by-pass but the splitting of a village and the creation of a permanent, offensive and subsequently useless scar.'

138 *The inner bypass, clearly visible in this aerial photograph, takes traffic away from the old centre but leaves the North Street area divided from the rest of the town. The Victoria Cottage Hospital (just above centre of photograph) has lost part of its grounds.*

139   *South Street in the 1950s. The decline of fishing and the long-term neglect of the buildings in this area left South Street looking drab and run-down in the post-war years.*

140   *South Street today. Renovation of the central area, which began in the 1960s, has made South Street one of the most attractive roads in the town.*

Several hundred residents signed a petition against the scheme in 1958 when the plan came before a public inquiry. The plan was, temporarily at least, shelved, but in the late 1960s it was revived. This time an Emsworth Short By-Pass Objection Committee was formed to fight the scheme, and when another public inquiry was held in 1970 Emsworth residents turned out in force: they came by coach, car and bus to show their 'contempt' for this new road. There was general agreement that the character of the town was being spoiled by traffic noise and pollution, but the solution, according to the objectors, was not to build a new short bypass road through the town, but to bring forward the plans which already existed for a longer bypass to the north of the railway line. To the dismay of the opposition, however, this 'ill-conceived road of destruction' (as one local correspondent to *The News* described it) was given planning approval by the Minister in 1971 and the battle was lost.

Since the 1970s both the short and long bypasses have been built and the centre of Emsworth – High Street and the Square – is free of through-traffic. On the other hand, the short bypass does to some extent form a physical barrier between the town centre and the North Street area. But the road has not split the community. The campaign to fight the road plan, which involved large numbers of local people in organising themselves, reinforced and strengthened the sense of community which has long been a feature of Emsworth. The determination to preserve Emsworth as a place with a unique character, based on its rich and varied history, has carried on and the town has experienced something of a renaissance in the past quarter of a century. Much, of course, has been lost. The King Street shipyard is now a housing development, but there is still boat building and repair within the town. There are no longer any working mills, but the buildings have been turned over to other uses and preserved as reminders of the town's past. The wrecks of old fishing smacks abandoned in

the harbour by J.D. Foster were finally removed in the 1970s, but not before there had been a campaign led by David Rudkin and others to preserve one of these vessels. Although the campaign was unsuccessful, it did lead directly to the establishment of the Emsworth Maritime and Historical Trust, a purely voluntary body made up of local people who have tirelessly and assiduously worked to preserve what remains of Emsworth's history. The Trust was able to acquire the old council offices in North Street in the 1980s and the Emsworth Museum was opened there in 1987.

A start was made in the 1960s on preserving the special character of the old centre of Emsworth: many of the old fishermen's cottages in the South Street area were renovated; the repainting of the façades of many buildings in the Square and the High Street brought some cosmetic improvements; the designation of the town centre as a Conservation Area in 1970, and the drawing up of an Emsworth Town Plan in the 1980s, including the listing of the many buildings which are of special architectural interest, have helped to preserve and enhance the town's fine architectural heritage; the creation of the Chichester Harbour Conservancy in 1971 marked a determination to preserve the unique ecology of the harbour and to regulate the many different activities within it. Local government reorganisation has, for administrative purposes, placed Emsworth within the borough of Havant, but, with a small swathe of green fields still separating Emsworth from its larger neighbour to the west, the town still retains its separate identity and its unique character.

A visitor to Emsworth today will encounter many reminders of the town's past: a silhouette of Foster's vessel, the *Echo*, has been adopted as the logo of the Emsworth Maritime and Historical Trust; the housing development in King Street has been called John King's Shipyard; and there are a number of references to oysters in the names of houses. Some of the shops in the High Street

141 *The Quay Mill in the 1970s. After decades of neglect and decay the mill building had become an eyesore on the Emsworth waterfront.*

142 *The Quay Mill after restoration. In 1979 the ESSC acquired the mill as the club's headquarters and extensive renovation work was undertaken. A modern fishing vessel is moored alongside the Town Quay.*

143   *Learning to sail. This 1980s photograph shows young people being taught to sail at the ESSC.*

144   *Hulks in Emsworth harbour, 1970s. The decayed hulk of the Ark is in the centre with the so-called* Echo II *alongside. Two more of Foster's vessels can be seen in advanced stages of decay. After the Chichester Harbour Conservancy was established in 1971 it was decided to remove the hulks because they represented a hazard to harbour users. Efforts by David Rudkin and others to preserve one of the vessels were unsuccessful, and their demolition was carried out by the Army.*

145 *Remains of oyster beds on Emsworth foreshore. At low tide it is still possible to see the stumps of the wooden posts that were used to build the oyster beds, and to pick up oyster shells.*

146 *Emsworth boatyard. Situated by the marina, this boatyard has the facilities to repair large modern sailing cruisers.*

147 *Aerial photograph of Emsworth. Despite the passage of time the lines of the old oyster beds and the shipyard slipway are still clearly visible in this photograph, taken at low tide. The triangular shape of the old marketplace (St Peter's Square) is still a characteristic feature of the centre of Emsworth. The entrance to the marina is just visible in the top left corner of the photograph.*

148 *Where it all began: Emsworth Square, after much renovation work over many years, provides an attractive focal point in the centre of the town. The cupola and clock on the former St Peter's Chapel now sit atop a restaurant.*

and the Square have been in the same families for generations. But Emsworth does not live in the past. In the early 21st century it is a thriving, vibrant community. The harbour still plays an important role in defining the town. With a large marina and two sailing clubs it is now better known for sailing than for fishing, although the latter still goes on. A small number of fishermen, some of whom belong to old established local

fishing families, still fish the grounds that have been worked by Emsworth fishermen for centuries. Fine seafood can be enjoyed in the many restaurants and the successful annual Food Festival brings many visitors to the place. All of these developments show that the strong sense of community and the spirit of enterprise which sustained Emsworth in the past are very much alive today.

Note on Sources

A. Primary sources

British Library (Newspaper Collection)
Hants and Sussex County Press, 1895-1957

Emsworth Maritime and Historical Trust (The Lewis Collection)
Headmaster's logbook, Washington Road School, 1898-1945
Oral history collection
'William Holloway' 1785-1870', Unpublished extracts from notebooks compiled by Stephen
    Holloway.

Hampshire Record Office
Catalogue of Prisoners, 1788-1847
Census Returns 1841-1901
Court Books of the Manor of Emsworth, 1686-1886
Havant Union Poor Law Guardians, Minute Books, 1856-1914
Trade Directories for Hampshire, 1792-1931
Warblington Urban District Council, Minute Books, 1899-1932
Warblington Urban District Council, Medical Officer of Health Reports, 1897-1914
Wills and probate records

Portsmouth Central Library
The Hampshire Telegraph, 1799-1926
The News, Portsmouth, 1935-1975

Portsmouth City Record Office
Foster Collection (Records of W. Foster &Co.)
Register of Shipping, 1824 1880
Crew Lists and Half-Yearly Agreements, 1858-1913
Parish Magazine, 1890-93
Warblington Parish, Select Vestry minute books, 1819-48
Warblington Parish, Overseers Account Books, 1823-36

B. SECONDARY SOURCES

R.J. Brooks, *Sussex Airfields in the Second World War* (1993)

W. Butler, *A Topographical History of the Hundred of Bosmere* (1817)

E. Carson, *Smugglers and Revenue Officers in the Portsmouth Area in the 18th Century* (Portsmouth Papers, 1973)

J. Chambers, *Hampshire Machine Breakers* (1996)

R. Coates, *The Place Names of Hampshire* (1989)

G. Daly, 'A Respectable Little Town' (Unpublished B.A. (Ports) Dissertation, 1999)

D. Defoe, *A Tour Through the Whole Island of Great Britain* (1996 ed.)

J. Farrant, *The Harbours of Sussex 1700-1914* (1976)

C. Frost, 'Tales from the Bar' (Unpublished history of Emsworth Slipper Sailing Club)

P. Haskell, *Ship Money in Hampshire* (Hampshire Studies, 1981)

A. Lambert, *Hants and Sussex* (1983)

C. Longcroft, *The Hundred of Bosmere* (1973 ed.)

P. Millen, *The Story of Emsworth Sailing Club* (1979)

V. Mitchell and K. Smith, *South Coast Railways – Chichester to Portsmouth* (1984)

R. and S. Morgan, *Inns, Taverns and Beerhouses* (Emsworth Papers, No. 1, 1994)

R. and S. Morgan, *P.G. Wodehouse and Emsworth* (Emsworth Papers, No. 2, 1994)

R. and S. Morgan, *Emsworth Square in 1840* (Emsworth Papers, No. 3, 1995)

R. and S. Morgan, *Religion in Emsworth* (Emsworth Papers, No. 4, 1996)

L. Newell, *Emsworth's Plum* (2004)

A.J.C. Reger, *A Short History of Emsworth and Warblington* (1967)

A.J.C. Reger, *Chichester Harbour, A History* (1996)

D. Rudkin, *The Hermitage and the Slipper* (1974)

D. Rudkin, *The Emsworth Oyster Fleet* (1975)

D. Rudkin, *Old Emsworth* (1978)

D. Rudkin, *The River Ems and Related Watercourses* (1984)

D. Rudkin, *Echo, The Queen of the Emsworth Oyster Fleet* (1987)

Victoria County History, *Hampshire and the Isle of Wight Vols. 1-3* (1900-8)

K. Vignoles, *St James's Church, Emsworth 1840-1990* (1990)

E. S. Washington, *Hampshire and the Catholic Revival of the 1580s* (Hamp 1981)

T. Yoward, *Emsworth Water Mills* (Emsworth Papers, No. 5, 2003)

T. Yoward, *Lumley Mill* (Hampshire Mills Group, 1999)

Index

References to illustrations are given in **bold**. Inns and vessels are shown in italics.